A MONTH AND A DAY
&
LETTERS

KEN SARO-WIWA

A MONTH AND A DAY
&
LETTERS

Foreword by

Wole Soyinka

ayebia

An Adinkra symbol meaning
Ntesie matemasie
A symbol of knowledge and wisdom

A Month And A Day & Letters © Ayebia Clarke Publishing Ltd
first published in 2005.

This edition of *A Month And A Day & Letters* published by
Ayebia Clarke Publishing Ltd in 2012
7 Syringa Walk
Banbury
Oxfordshire
OX16 1FR
UK
www.ayebia.co.uk

The Paperback edition of *A Month And A Day* was first published in 1995
by Penguin Books.

Distributed outside Africa, Europe and the United Kingdom
and exclusively in the US by
Lynne Rienner Publishers Inc
1800 30th Street, Suite 314
Boulder, CO 80301
USA
www.rienner.com

Distributed in the UK and Europe by *TURNAROUND* Publisher Services,
Wood Green, London, UK, www.turnaround-uk.com

Distributed in Southern Africa by Book Promotions a subsidiary of Jonathan Ball
Publishers in South Africa. For orders contact: jbpcapetown@jonathanball.co.za
and orders@bookpro.co.za

British Library Cataloguing-in-Publication Data.
A catalogue record of this book is available from the British Library

Cover Design by Amanda Carroll at Millipedia, Chesham,UK.
Cover photograph of Ken Saro-Wiwa reproduced by kind permission of
Greenpeace/Lambon
Typeset by FiSH Books, Enfield, Middlesex, UK.
Printed and bound in Great Britain by CPI-Cox & Wyman Ltd., Reading, Berkshire.

ISBN 978-0-9547023-5-9

Available from www.ayebia.co.uk or email info@ayebia.co.uk

The Publisher wishes to acknowledge the support of
Arts Council England SE Funding.

Contents

---

*First published in *In the Shadow of a Saint*, Transworld Publishers, UK, 2000

ACKNOWLEDGEMENTS

PUTTING this book together has been a collaborative effort in the truest sense of the word. In its second incarnation, each time these prison diaries have been posthumously published has required the faith of professionals with a moral core – Becky Ayebia Clarke, the Publisher, who so believed in this project that she was prepared to retype the entire manuscript, before Penny Ormerod, the Editor, pared it down from the original published but raw identity. Thanks, too, to Caroline Sinclair for her careful checking of the text, and to the Designers, Amanda Carroll and Rob Craig.

Beyond that hard labour of love there were many other co-consiprators: Makin Soyinka, Dr. Owens Wiwa, Olivia Wiwa, Sister Majella McCarron, Sara Whyatt at PEN, Mandy Garner at THES (*Times Higher Education Supplement*), Ursula Owen and Judith Vidal-Hall at Index on Censorship and Professor Wole Soyinka. Their encouragement and contributions pushed this over the finishing line.

Then there are the others: the Ogoni people – and the hundreds of thousands, millions of people who have given their support to my father, and the cause of justice in Nigeria and social justice globally. This is their story too. So on behalf of my father, my family, our people, we thank you.

Ken Wiwa,
12 November 2005

FOREWORD

Flight from Auckland – November 1995

I WAS due in Tokyo, Japan, but not for a number of days. I diverted to Auckland where the Commonwealth Heads of States were gathering for their biannual summit; and it was clear that they alone, at that stage, still commanded the weight of voices that might save nine innocent men from the gallows. My message was insistent, desperate and even strident: *only strong threats will save these lives; strong threats backed by unmistakable indications that such threats will be enforced if the sentence is carried out!* Occasionally, very exceptionally, I encountered an adviser who listened and thought hard and deep, as if resolved to influence attitudes within his delegation or the routine caucuses. I then walked back into the sunlit streets, desperately plucking courage from such meagre signs.

The day's brightness augured well, but beneath it cautioned the persistent voice of the life-battered character, Mama Put, from my play, *The Beatification of Area Boy,* which had just begun its run at the West Yorkshire Playhouse, Leeds, England. The coincidences were unnerving. Mama Put was a fugitive from the Delta region, the same embattled oil founts of Ken Saro-Wiwa and the Ogoni people. As if strolling beside me, her voice continued to resound in my head, straight from the rehearsals:

A sky such as this brings no good with it. The clouds have vanished from the sky but, where are they? In the hearts of those below. In the rafters. Over the hearth. Blighting the vegetable patch. Slinking through the orange grove. Rustling the plantain leaves and withering them – oh, I heard them again last night – and poisoning the fishponds. When the gods mean to be kind to us, they draw up the gloom to themselves – yes, a cloud is a good sign, only, not many people know that. Even a wisp, a mere shred of cloud over my roof would bring me comfort, but not this stark, cruel brightness. It's not natural. It's a deceit.

The Beatification of Area Boy was a play I had written long before Ken's travails – indeed, it was to have commenced rehearsals in Nigeria a mere week or so before I was compelled to flee the country. Now Mama Put appeared to have taken on Ken Saro-Wiwa's voice from his dungeon. She was speaking of the Nigerian Civil War – one in which, again as it happened, Ken had played an important role. Like a night bird perched on my head, Mama Put continued to intone Ken's indictment of his latest adversaries – the oil companies and their military collaborators in the Nigerian nation:

Those who did this thing to us, those who turned our fields of garden eggs and prize tomatoes into mush, pulp and putrid flesh... After the massacre of our youth came the plague of oil rigs and the new death of farmland, shrines and fish sanctuaries, and the eternal flares that turn night into day and blanket the land with globules of soot...

Jerked back into the present of Auckland masquerading as a clone of my hometown, Abeokuta, my mind grasping greedily at distractions, I wondered, absurdly, if the successful preservation of the woodlands of New Zealand had anything to do with the prominent role of New Zealanders in the wave of ecological championing then sweeping across the globe. And, sure enough, later that morning, I came upon a demonstration organised in denunciation of the British Prime Minister, John Major – expected at the conference – for his support of the French atomic explosion being carried out in the South Pacific islands, despite a near-unanimous condemnation by the world.

The demonstration, I soon observed, was beamed at multiple

targets. When the crowd came to an open space, it stopped, and a street drama began, utilising huge satirical masks. One of the themes dealt with the social injustices under which the Maoris, the original owners of the land, still laboured in modern-day New Zealand. I thought – aah, this would have been meat and drink to Ken! He would have mounted the rostrum, his trademark pipe to the fore, pugnacious, and . . . suddenly, there he was, larger than life! Banners were unfurled and I saw Ken Saro-Wiwa hoisted high up above the trees and shopping malls: NO WAY FOR NIGERIAN DICTATORS! FREE KEN SARO-WIWA! SHELL IS HELL! OIL FOR BLOOD? It was a most uplifting moment, a morale booster that brought the talkative birds back into the sunlight, routing the owls and offals of the preceding night's fitful sleep.

But they returned. They came back when no-one was watching, taking up patient positions in ironic response to the up-beat mood of the politicians. For these would hear of no alarms, dismissed all notion of deadly peril. No-one, they said, would dare hang those men – and, again, the magic mantra – hadn't Sanni Abacha personally given his word to Nelson Mandela? The sentence would not be endorsed by the all-powerful Ruling Council – you wait and see. What? Hang them in defiance of world opinion? And while the Commonwealth Summit is taking place? Really, Mr Soyinka, don't you think this is – no offence meant, you understand, I don't mean this personally – but really that is over-dramatising the situation. Sanni Abacha merely wants to give them a fright!

The junior Ken and I joined forces on some of these visits, or else our paths crossed in hotel lobbies, our faces heavy with foreboding. Looking back, I can see what a dreary contrast we made to the buoyant smiles that wreathed the faces of Ministers of Foreign Affairs, Heads of States and Ambassadors – African, European or Asian. I was saddened, not angry, because it was clear that they could not understand. They had never encountered, nor studied a creature of Sanni Abacha's cast of mind. It was my cast of mind that they found abnormal, the more I tried to wear them down with the brutality of my conviction: *If you fail to act, that man is going to hang Ken!*

Today, even after the tragic *denouement*, I am mildly surprised to find, it is not anger or bitterness that I feel as my mind traverses the few years; only sadness, tinged of course with renewed pain, as I recall the responses of those leaders. In the main – these Heads of States of the Commonwealth – former colonies of Great Britain, from Canada through Asia and Africa to Australia – few, despite their varied experience of humanity, had ever encountered, except in history books, the likes of Sanni Abacha. Maybe, even now, they still believe that Hitler, Stalin and Pol Pot were all mutants, created perhaps by undetected spores that spilled out of some secret Chernobyl, or the singular gas seepage from our neighbouring Cameroon's Lake Nyos that killed, in the 1980s, hundreds of sleeping victims between night and dawn. They conveniently forgot the lesson of Idi Amin Dada within their own club of nations. Their Foreign Ministers, ambassadors, advisers, political analysts *et al* were mostly creatures of bloodless briefings, of cynical lobbies, of cocktail and diplomatic reception circuits where the formal attire is camouflage for both viper and dove, and records of atrocities are shed at the door, with a crested visiting card. The rest, like the rulers they served, were potential clones of the Abacha breed, and simply wondered what the fuss was all about.

I *knew* Sanni Abacha – no, not personally, though we had met twice. It was simply his type that I knew intimately, a species that I had studied closely, lectured and written about. I did not share the confidence of the others, but I was hopeful – at least, at the start. And it was just as well. We were all doomed to be eviscerated by an invisible blade wielded by a psychopath from a place called Abuja. My only saving grace was that I had already felt its thrust, long before the noose tightened around Kenule's neck.

Four Ogoni chiefs in the Niger Delta had been murdered, denounced as collaborators with the military government and the oil companies. These were brutal, horrendous killings, totally indefensible. To the extent that the murders had been committed by Ogoni youth militants, members of MOSOP – e Movement for the Survival of the Ogoni People – who

owed loyalty to Ken Saro-Wiwa, their leader, and that he failed to condemn the murders in the most rigorous language, Ken could be assailed with a measure of *moral* responsibility. But to accuse him of complicity, direct or indirect, was an act of cynical opportunism. To convict him and his companions in a hastily convened military court, and on the 'evidence' placed before the nation, was an act of minds totally devoid of all conscience, perhaps steeped in a diabolism that required human sacrifice. And finally, to proceed to hang those victims, before they had exhausted all channels of appeal that were open to them even within the provisions of the decree that established the 'judicial process', was a step that no sensate person ever thought possible – from the Ogoni infant in his village, to the sage Nelson Mandela who arrived at Auckland airport beaming with confidence and dismissing the anxious questions of journalists with a jovial wave of the hand. Had Abacha not personally assured him, in a telephone exchange, that he would not execute those men?

Even now, I still relive those moments of intense isolation, leaving one truly 'spaced out' – spaced out, as in spinning in outer space – an alien among supportive, courteous mortals, yet with a feeling that clung to you; that, among the teeming population of that island, you were one of the mere handful of creatures – no more than two or three, one of whom was Ken's son – who knew, with absolute certainty, that a mass murder was about to be committed; yet you were powerless to stop it or persuade anyone to believe you. My final moment of certitude came from a chance crossing of paths.

On the streets of Auckland, where I exorcised my restlessness and frustration with incessant walking, between appointments, a car drew up with young Ken, the son of the condemned man, and some workers from the Body Shop and other NGOs who were looking after him. Ken leapt out, thrust a cyclostyled statement from the Shell Company. If ever there was a scripted form of Pontius Pilate washing his hands before handing Christ over to his executioners, this would be its very corporate equivalent! *If anything untoward happened to the Ogoni Nine,* the statement declared, *others were to blame –*

the agitators whose aggressive tactics only hardened the mood of the military regime and undid all the careful work of silent diplomacy being undertaken by their company, and well-meaning others.

Yes, *we* were to blame, not Shell! Not the oil exploration companies. Not the military regime, its corporate allies, its kangaroo courts, but we! I handed back this tract of self-exoneration, of company unctuousness and – it seemed clear to me – accessory knowledge. In my distraction, I thought I had spoken aloud and flagellated myself long afterwards for an outburst that was wrung out of me without consideration for the son's presence. But he assured me, much later, that I had the sequence of events all wrong. For what I thought I had blurted out without thinking was: *He's dead. They've decided to hang them. This statement – Shell knows of the decision already.* Even today, however, the words still ring in my head as I thought I heard them, clear as the tolling of a funeral bell.

Walking myself into a state of total exhaustion from a sweaty pace around the humid streets of Auckland, mostly along the harbour, beginning to feel somewhat dizzy, and recognising why – I had had only my usual morning espresso that day – I entered a restaurant off the beaten track where I attempted to stuff my insides; but again, mostly drank. Then, instead of returning to the hotel, I went to the improvised office of the Body Shop NGO – it was abandoned, the volunteers were between hotels, waylaying and canvassing whatever delegates they could. I knew why I remained there, in that abandoned office – it was to await the news. I did not wish to be found, did not wish to be invited to join in canvassing one more statesman or delegate. I returned to my hotel room only when it was late, and news of the confirmation of sentence by Abacha's military ruling council had been formally announced.

Now I had only one thought – to get out of New Zealand! I had an engagement in Japan – a gathering of Nobel Laureates – but we were not expected for two more days. That was just too bad. I sent a message, but did not really care whether or not I was not met, or if I upset the protocols that appear to be encoded in the national genes of the Japanese. I had only one goal in mind – to escape the island that would shortly host a wake for complacent Heads of States, their political advisers and their pundits. They would fashion statements of indignation and perform other accustomed rites of assaulted dignity – that would be their problem, it was no longer mine. The statement from Shell may not have been a death warrant, but it was so clearly a death certificate that I no longer thought of Ken as being in the world of the living, and I had no wish to encounter politicians and statesmen after the event. Above all, I most certainly did not wish to speak to the press...*So what is your view on these executions, Mr. Soyinka?* Finally, I did not wish to witness the agony of a son when the now inevitable hole in his life yawned before him. All these sent me looking for the next plane out of Auckland, heading in the direction of Tokyo where I knew I would have a clear two days alone before I was again obliged to face the world.

I obtained relief from this irrational dread of pursuit only when the plane was airborne and out of New Zealand airspace. Arrived in Tokyo, ensconced in a temporary suite by my polite hosts, I awaited the expected.

It came in the morning, in the form of a young journalist, ushered into my suite by a geisha-attired woman who had been specially assigned to look after me, sitting just outside my room at all times – I later discovered – as if my hosts from *Shinbum*, the publishing house, feared that I might go into depression, do some kind of harm to myself. Ken Saro-Wiwa, and his eight companions, the young man said, had been hanged in Port Harcourt prisons, shortly after the rejection of their appeal by the Supreme Military Council of Sanni Abacha.

Never were hosts more gentle, more sensitive, self-retiring yet solicitous. The editor of the newspaper house, sponsors of the conference, called on me. His brief stay was virtually soundless. In the most delicate manner, he indicated that the contents of the envelope that he was leaving on the table were for me to use in any way I wanted; that it was a gift of sympathy from his fellow executives who wished to ensure that I lacked nothing, yet were conscious of my likely preference to be alone. If I wished to look round the city, however, I need only inform the lady by the door and she would get in touch with his office. Even the choice of the young journalist who broke the news could not have been more deft. He looked more like a medical intern with practised bedside manners, tried to hide his astonishment (and relief) that I took the news so well. How was he to know that I had prepared myself, that I had left Auckland wondering only how soon the killing would be carried out! He tiptoed his way out, saying that he knew I would wish to be alone. Not that he forgot his calling - he left his card on the table by the door – if at any time, I wished to make a statement, he would remain on call.

Being prepared for the worst is always one thing; confronting its stark actualisation is another. There is a point at which the mind threatens to fold up, succumbing to its own destructive power of evocation... how does one erase the image of a friend and comrade, suspended in the immense loneliness of a prison yard? This was more harrowing than the mere degradation of land: my human landscape had become irremediably desecrated.

Wole Soyinka

From *You Must Set Forth At Dawn* – forthcoming Memoirs. Delivered by the author on Wednesday, 9 November 2005, Purcell Room, Royal Festival Hall, South Bank London on the occasion of the 10th Anniversary, Remembering Ken Saro-Wiwa Campaign.

PART I

A Month and a Day
A Detention Diary
21 June–22 July 1993

PREFACE

I HAD completed the first draft of this book when, on 21 May 1994, two of the men to whom I give a lot of attention, Mr Albert Badey and Chief Edward Kobani, were cruelly murdered along with two other prominent Ogoni men at Giokoo in Ogoni. That gruesome and sad event altered my original story somewhat but has not made material difference to it. My condolences go to the bereaved families.

It will be no surprise to my readers to know that the Movement for the Survival of the Ogoni People (MOSOP) was accused of the crime in which I suspect the Nigerian security agencies had a hand. I was promptly arrested, along with the rest of the leadership of MOSOP, and I have since been in leg cuffs in a secret military camp outside Port Harcourt, where I have been held incommunicado and been tortured, mentally and physically.

The ten months from 22 July 1993, when the incidents narrated in this book end, to 22 May 1994, when I was again arrested and detained, were very difficult for the Ogoni people and the events of that period would have enriched this book even more. However, given the fact that I am not certain what the immediate future may bring, I have thought it wise to get my original draft published, and have therefore smuggled it into my detention cell and am correcting and redrafting it in very difficult circumstances.

I should add that I have used the term 'Ogoni' in preference to 'Ogoniland', which is fast becoming current; this is because to the Ogoni, the land and the people are one and are expressed as such in our local languages. It emphasises, to my mind, the close relationship between the Ogoni people and their environment.

Ken Saro-Wiwa
Port Harcourt
July 1994

Chapter One

SUDDENLY, my car screeched to a halt. I raised my head in surprise. Before me was an armed security man flagging the car down, his rifle pointing at my chauffeur's head. Then, just as suddenly, more security men in mufti headed for the rear door of the car, swung it open, and ordered me to get down. I refused. They spoke more gruffly and I remained just as adamant. A superior officer whom I knew well ordered two of the men to get into the empty front seat of the car. They obeyed him. Then they ordered my chauffeur to do a U-turn against the traffic. He obeyed. The security officer had turned his own car around and ordered my chauffeur to follow him. Behind us was yet another car which I knew to be a security vehicle crammed with security men. We drove off in a convoy.

It was 21 June 1993. We were at a crossroads in Port Harcourt, at the busy UTC junction on the equally busy expressway linking the city with the town of Aba to the north. The drama took place in front of commuters, and I imagine that many would have guessed that I was being arrested. I, however, knew it for sure. It was my fourth arrest in three months.

As we drove towards the Port Harcourt Club Sports Ground, there was no doubt in my mind as to where we were going: the scrappy offices of the State Security Service (SSS), where I was already a well-known customer, as the saying goes in Nigeria. I chuckled to myself.

When we got to the walled-off compound of the dreaded SSS, I got out of my car and instructed my chauffeur to return to my office and let everyone know that I was under arrest. The security men did not impede his departure. They had more urgent matters on their minds.

There was a flurry of activity, a running up and down the stairs by the most senior of my captors, and no-one bothered much what I was doing with myself. On previous occasions, I would have engaged in a banter with the young security agents. This time round, I sensed that matters had become more serious and there was not much to joke about. There was an ominous air blowing through the building, once a beautiful place surrounded by a well-manicured lawn, but now generally run-down and grubby. In a short while, the officer who had run upstairs returned, waving a piece of paper. I was ordered into the back of one of the waiting cars, between two gruff and unsmiling security men. We drove out of the SSS compound.

In ten minutes we were at the Central Police Station, a place with which I was not unfamiliar. It had been the state headquarters of the Nigerian Police Force but when the Force's new office buildings were complete, it was turned over to the State Intelligence and Investigation Bureau (SIIB). It was, as usual with public property in Nigeria, in disrepair. The lawn was littered with cars, in difference colours and states. Some appeared to have been there for ages, waiting to be used as exhibits for cases that would never be tried.

I was ushered into a little cubicle which served as office for some investigating police officers, and asked to sit on a wooden bench. I sat there chewing on the stem of my pipe while one of the investigating police officers, who was taking down a statement from an accused person, stared incredulously at me. I had been very much in the news lately, and, as often happens to those who have the misfortune, was considered more as a news item than as a living being with flesh and blood.

In another 15 minutes a form was pushed in front of me and I was asked to write a statement about my activities on Election Day, 12 June 1993. The Ogoni, under leadership of the Movement for the Survival of the Ogoni People (MOSOP), had boycotted the election. I asked perfunctorily to be allowed to see my lawyer before committing myself to paper. The request, as I expected, was turned down. Without further ado, I whipped out my pen and wrote the required statement, knowing full well that it would never be used. I signed it with a flourish.

A beautiful young woman, a senior police officer, soon came in to examine the statement I had written. She read it, seemed satisfied, and then offered me a place on a rickety wooden chair in her curtained office next door. She disappeared with the statement. I was left to my pipe. I stoked it, lit it, and drew deeply. My mind flew about like a bird on a wing.

The young lady returned and engaged me in conversation. We spoke about Nigeria, about the suffering of the peoples of Rivers State, of oil and the sorrows it had brought those on whose land it is found, of the social inequalities in this country, of oppression and all such. She was an Izon, neighbours of the Ogoni and the fourth largest ethnic group of Nigeria's 200-odd groups; they live in the main oil-producing area of the country. She fully understood all the arguments I had been making and certainly sympathised with them and with me for the travail I had suffered in recent months. She assured me, like many operatives I have met, and am yet to meet, that she did not mean any harm to me but that she was only doing her duty. I accepted her assertions graciously.

This conversation took the sting out of the waiting hour. She soon left the room and her place was taken by a middle-aged man who introduced himself as the husband of the young officer. He also engaged me in a conversation similar to that of his wife. In this way did I spend another 30 minutes.

The lady returned to the room and asked me to accompany her to the main buildings. As we crossed the open courtyard with its litter of cars, a bird whispered to me that I was to be taken into detention in Lagos. Nothing that I did not expect. I was beginning to steel myself for any eventuality. It was only then that it occurred to me that I had not had a meal the whole day.

We climbed the dark, dingy steps of the main building to the first floor and I was led before another senior police officer in flowing cotton robes. He offered me a seat from his work table and I sat there while there was a considerable to-ing and fro-ing of other police officers, including the man who had played a leading role in my abduction on the expressway. They whispered conspiratorially to the senior police officer and he whispered orders back to them. I watched them with an amused look. Had I known exactly what they were planning, I doubt that I would have found it funny.

After what seemed like an interminable wait, the senior police officer told me that on Election Day, 12 June 1993, policemen had been made to frog-march people in Ogoni and there had been disturbances. I told him that was news to me, as I had been in Lagos, 1,000 kilometres away, and nowhere near Ogoni on the day in question. That did not impress him. He then told me that I was under arrest. I thanked him for the information.

A longish silence followed while I digested this. I looked round the room. It was large – big enough for a huge writing-desk and a full complement of cushioned chairs and two or three filing cabinets. The man at the desk, I noticed, was pencil-thin with aquiline features.

'I gather you're sending me to Lagos.'

'Who told you?'

'A bird.'

'What?'

'The wind.'

'I am not sending you to Lagos.'

Liar. I wanted to hit him on his lying lips. I pulled out my pipe, struck a match and drew. The smoked danced into the air, upwards towards the ceiling.

'I haven't had anything to eat all day,' I said.

He drew a kola nut from the folds of his dress, broke it in two and offered me half. I declined. He bit into his half and crunched away. I blew more smoke into the air.

My stomach was grumbling like hell. 'I need to eat,' I said. 'We're making arrangements to get you your food,' he replied.

He got up and walked slowly out of the room, and I was left to my thoughts. Injustice stalks the land like a tiger on the prowl. To be at the mercy of buffoons is the ultimate insult. To find the instruments of state power reducing you to dust is the injury.

Perforce, my mind went back to the events of that afternoon. I had been at my office with the usual collection of Ogoni youths discussing the events of the election, which the Ogoni people had decided to boycott. I had not been present in Ogoni during the elections. Now, Ogoni youths were filling me in on the details of the boycott. As we talked, one of my security guards came to inform me that a man he suspected to be from the SSS had come calling and he had told him that I was not available. The man had gone away, but he felt sure that he had not gone far. He would, as was their wont, hang around till my car showed up. He would then barge into my office. I thanked the guard and continued to listen to the men in my office.

A while afterwards my chauffeur returned, and, as the security guard had informed me, five men walked into my office behind him without bothering to knock on the door. I recognised one of them as a security agent. They were all in mufti. I greeted the man whom I recognised cheerily and he smiled. We knew what it was all about, by routine.

'Oga wants to see you, sir,' he said, meaning that I was being summoned by his boss, the state director of the SSS. 'Sorry, I'm not available,' I replied.

'But, sir…'

'You know I have a high court injunction restraining you from infringing my fundamental human rights. It's not as it was in the past. Now, before you arrest me, you have to produce a warrant. You can't just barge into my office or tap me on the shoulder on the highway or at the airport and expect me to follow you. Do you have a warrant of arrest?'

'We haven't come to arrest you. We're only inviting you to the office.'

'To drink tea or have lunch?'

'Just come along with us,' pleaded the robust black man whom I hadn't seen before. He had perfect dentition, I observed.

'No, I'm sorry, I can't come with you.' This, with finality.

The altercation went on longer. And when they found that I was adamant, they trooped out of my office. The Ogoni youths advised me to leave. But I knew better and we continued our discussion.

Fifteen minutes later the security agents, all four or five of them, returned armed with a warrant of arrest. They presented me with it. I read it and noted that it was signed by a Mrs Aguma, Justice of the Peace. It stated expressly that the security agents were free to search my premises and if anything incriminating were found, I was to be brought before her court. I latched on to this and offered to go with them to Mrs Aguma's court and not to the SSS office.

The security agent had not read the warrant, and he took it from me and read it now before me. Then he pocketed it.

'You're making our work difficult for us,' said one of them. 'Just come with us to the office. There is nothing in it.'

'I have a court injunction. But if you like, I'll call in at your office later today. Say, six o'clock. Only as a matter of courtesy. I have a meeting at 2 pm.' I looked at my watch. It was already 2.15 pm. 'Oh dear, I'm late. And I don't like to go late to meetings!'

'All right, sir, 'said one of them. 'We're leaving.' And they walked out of my office.

I tidied my desk, left my briefcase on my table and went downstairs into my car. As I opened my car door, a busload of

9

policemen drove into the bus stop in front of my office. The fact that they drove against the normal flow of traffic, that the bus was new and did not bear the usual insignia of the Nigerian Police Force, made me suspicious. But I did not give further thought to it.

My office in Port Harcourt lies on the busy Aggrey Road in the centre of the old township, which had been very well laid out by the colonial government before the Nigerian military came to ruin it with their disorderliness and incompetence. No-one wreaked more havoc on the layout of the old township than Governor Diete-Spiff, a navy officer who was appointed to office by the Gowon administration in 1967 upon the creation of Rivers State in that year. He proceeded to turn every open space created by the original planners of the town into a building lot. And by the time subsequent rulers of the state had stopped collecting garbage and cleaning the gutters, old Port Harcourt had become another slum. Because my office gave out on to Aggrey Road, I did not get the full effect of the slum quality of the town. There was a bus stop pat in front of the office, so I often found unsolicited entertainment of the street variety if I peeped through the window, or as I came in and went out.

But that afternoon I was not in search of entertainment. I was, myself, providing much of it. So, driving out of the place was a welcome development. A large number of Ogoni youths, anxious to protect me from the security agents, had gathered, and some of them insisted they would come with me in the car, just in case. But I told them that I had no need for company. I did take a lawyer with me in the car, but that was to offer him a lift. As soon as we got to his chambers, I dropped him off and continued alone towards the venue of the meeting of Ogoni elders; they had been most affected by the boycott of the elections and were licking their wounds, threatening fire and brimstone against all who did not see eye to eye with them. I had hoped that the meeting would help assuage their fears and worries.

10

I had calculated that the meeting was going to last three to four hours and that, at its conclusion, I would report to the SSS at about 6 pm. So I planned.

What I did not know, and what I should have known, was that the security agents were not being sincere when they had said that they would be leaving me. I hardly thought that they would be waylaying me on a busy thoroughfare at 2.45 pm and that by 6.30 pm I would be the guest of a fidgety, lying Assistant Commissioner of Police.

My host soon returned to his office, and this time he appeared a bit panicky. He picked up a walkie-talkie, put it back in its place, called his man Friday, asked for another walkie-talkie, found it impossible to operate the same, sat in his seat, looked out of the window, went back to the door, stepped out of the office, returned to the room and to his seat, and chewed on his kola nut.

At that point young Barry Kumbe from Ledum Mitee's chambers, my lawyers, asked to see the Assistant Commissioner of Police. The latter turned down the request. I pleaded with him to allow me to speak to Barry. He would not allow it. I said I wanted at least to have someone tell my household of my whereabouts and possibly arrange a meal for me. My captor was unrelenting. I asked to use the lavatory. Permission granted.

On the way back from the hallowed ground, which was not kept neat at all, Barry Kumbe waylaid me. I informed him that I thought I might be taken to Lagos and asked him to make all the arrangements for my legal defence, if that was going to be of any use whatsoever.

I was still speaking with Barry when my captor arrived and ordered the former to go away. I returned to the room.

Night was already falling and I was roaring hungry.

'Have you really made arrangements for my dinner?' I asked.

He became impatient. 'Don't worry,' he said, 'we know our

work.' I watched him as he chewed on his kola nut. To stay the anger that was welling up in me, I had to have recourse to my pipe. There was continuous motion in the room as police officers came and went, conferring with their boss, as earlier on, in low conspiratorial tones. The slow minutes ticked by. I wondered what was in store for me.

At eight o'clock or thereabouts my medical doctor brother, Owens, was announced. This time, my captor had no hesitation in allowing him in. He then went out and allowed me and my brother to be alone. The Nigerian police hate lawyers. They do not mind doctors. Lesson learnt.

Owens and I share the same birthday, 10 October, 14 years apart. He was at first the most apolitical of men. After qualifying from medical school at the University of Calabar, he had worked for a brief time in the Rivers State Ministry of Health and, when he found that constricting, set up a clinic at Bori, the headquarters of the Ogoni. Without electricity or telephone or pipe-borne water, the practice was not satisfactory and the misery all around was virtually unbearable. And I believe that this was what turned him into a tireless political activist.

When we started the Movement for the Survival of the Ogoni People, it took him some time to assess the organisation. But by 4 January 1993, when we had the mammoth protest march involving about 300,000 people which signalled the commencement of the non-violent resistance to our denigration as a people, he had become a key factor in the movement. On the day of the march he was one of the few medical practitioners around, and the ambulance belonging to his clinic was the only vehicle available to take care of any emergency cases.

He walked into the room with a bundle of currency notes, a toothbrush and paste and some medicine. Most thoughtful of him, I noted gratefully.

'As I was coming upstairs, someone at the reception advised me to give you enough medicine to last you a long time.'

We laughed.

'I understand I'm to be taken to Lagos. There's no aircraft tonight, so it's likely to be tomorrow. Meanwhile, I haven't had a bite all day. Can you arrange to get me something from my place?'

My brother soon departed and, after a while, the Assistant Commissioner of Police arrived and motioned to me to follow him. We went through the dimly lit corridor and down the short staircase to the ground floor. There, stationed and waiting, was a vehicle I was to become more than familiar with over the next month and a day, a Peugeot J5 passenger bus.

I was ordered into the bus. As I climbed in, a gentleman in a lounge suit ordered me to put out my unlit pipe. I quickly pocketed it. Another police office in a Yoruba-style kaftan and trousers seized my packet of matches. My stomach roared.

The bus held several plastic jerry cans of petrol, there being a general shortage in the country at the time. The bus itself reeked of the smell of petrol and I felt like puking. I steeled myself. The mere thought of driving in the vehicle was enough to upset me. I hadn't travelled to Lagos by road for 20 years or more. Eight armed police climbed into the bus after me. In the front seat were the man in a lounge suit and another man, whom I presumed to be a senior police officer. The man in the kaftan sat next to me on one of the padded seats. I noticed that there was a pick-up van also full of armed policemen in front of the bus. And standing about were policemen armed with riot gear. In a few minutes, in a hail of tear gas, we were on our way out of the compound.

We drove into Aggrey Road, past my office. I noticed a small crowd had gathered in front, all of them wearing anxious faces. I looked at my watch. It was 10.30 pm. If we were going to Lagos, I thought, we would have to drive all night. My heart beat a wild tattoo. Why, I asked myself, would the police want to put me through such torture?

The bus sped through the heart of Port Harcourt, on to the

13

Port Harcourt – Aba Expressway, and towards Rumuo-kwuta junction. The normally busy road lay quiet, although a few vehicles still plied it. Once out of Port Harcourt, the lights of the houses disappeared from sight and the headlights of the vehicle picked up the bushes as we rushed past.

The man in the lounge suit put me at a considerable ease when he said, 'Mr Saro-Wiwa, I know you well by reputation. I have read a lot of your newspaper articles. But more than that, your wife and mine were together at Imaguero College in Benin in the1970s.'

'Really!' I exclaimed. 'Isn't it a small world? And what's your name?'

'Don't worry about that.'

'Where are we going to?'

'Don't worry. When we get there, you'll know.'

'Why do we have to drive at night? Am I safe?'

'Don't worry. At least you know you're in the hands of the police. You're safe.'

What comfort. The hands of the police offer safety and protection? The Nigerian Police? Aren't they the ones who've shot people at check-points? Isn't it in their custody cells that accused persons regularly die? What protection could the police offer against a motor accident? What if armed robbers were to waylay the convoy and there was a shoot-out? A myriad of uncomfortable thoughts crossed my mind.

I had in my hand only my black clutch-bag crammed with my tobacco, diary, address book, calculator, scissors for cutting and a pencil. I also had some 2,000 Naira* which my brother Owens had thoughtfully given me at the police station. The thought of armed robbers made me hold my clutch-bag tightly. For a fleeting moment, I thought of the possibility of the policemen who were with me pounding on me and taking away the money. I dismissed the thought just as quickly.

The bus sped on through the night on the narrow tarmac road that led towards Warri in the west. In the brief

---

*130 Naira is approximately US$1

14

conversation which I held with the man in the lounge suit, I gathered that he had attended the University of Ibadan, where he had read history, and the University of Lagos, where he had read law. He was therefore no ordinary police officer. Somehow, I felt a bit more comfortable knowing that I was in the hands of a man of some education.

Throughout the journey I did not sleep a wink. I knew the road to Warri well enough, having just done the trip in early April when I had been slated to give a lecture to the National Association of Itsekiri Students.

On that occasion I had driven in the comfort of my new air-conditioned car. The road through Izon country had been rough and so had the journey. I arrived in Warri to the welcoming hand of 20 police officers and men who had been detailed to arrest me on arrival. They promptly did so before I had had the opportunity of informing the students that I was in Warri. They took me to the police station, searched my bags and ordered me out of the town.

For good measure, they escorted me out of Delta State, in which Warri lies, stationing a senior police officer in my car to ensure that I did not escape, while another car full of police officers led the way. They dumped me on the other side of the Niger River in my home state, Rivers State, and bid me goodbye with a smile. I had been quite safe in the hands of the police.

Warri was as silent as a graveyard when we arrived there. My captors had meant, I understood from the conversation which followed, to stop at one of the police stations in the town in order to catch some sleep. In the event, they could not find their way and we had to stop at a petrol-filling station.

Everyone except myself went to sleep. I thought then of my youth and how I might have been tempted, in those heady days, to jump out of the bus, grab a rifle from one of the sleeping guards and shoot my way to safety or to adventure and death. I thought also, for a brief moment, of my family: my father, mother, brothers, sister, and how they would be

15

feeling. I thought of my children: he that was ill in my house in Port Harcourt; and of that other one, the elegant young boy, 14 years old, whom I had buried only in March..

But my main thought went to the Ogoni people and the travails they had been forced to endure for over a century, which travail I was determined as iron to mitigate in my lifetime. I thought of the tremendous courage they had shown in the six months since I began to stir up things and to raise the questions which no-one seemed willing to confront. I wondered what they would do, faced as they were with my arrest.

They were unused to political activism and the dangers inherent in it. I had taken them on a hard journey and although I had prepared their minds for it in public speeches and in private, I was not quite sure how they would react in any particular circumstance. Some were used to the detention endured by mostly Yoruba activists in Nigeria. None of their kin had ever undergone such horrors. They had been sleepwalking their way towards extinction, not knowing what internal colonialism had done and was doing to them. It had fallen to me to wake them up from the sleep of the century, and I had accepted in full the responsibility for doing so. Would they be able to stand up to the rigours of the struggle?

I was to learn later that Ogoni youths had shown far more solidarity, far more courage, than I had credited them with. Not knowing what happened to me, they had gone in a group of 500 or more to the offices of the SSS and opened every single door in an effort to trace me. And when they had not found me there, they had gone to the Central Police Station in Port Harcourt, where they engaged the riot police in a struggle. They picked up canisters of tear gas shot by the police before they could explode and threw them back at their tormentors. They tore down a part of the brick wall which fenced off the police station from the rest of the town. And almost all night they lit bonfires along Aggrey Road to place a distance between the brutality of the police and themselves. They made sure that the town of Port Harcourt heard their protest at my arrest.

Meanwhile, at four o'clock, my captors roused themselves from their sleep and we recommenced our journey. While we were stationary, the inside of the bus was quite stuffy. As we began to drive, fresh air streamed in and I felt refreshed, if not invigorated.

We drove on in silence, past sleepy little villages nestling close to the engulfing forest, over a bumpy tarmac road, towards Benin City.

The state of the road irked me. It was one of my overriding concerns. Not the road itself, but the fact that in this rich, oil-bearing area, the roads should be so rickety, while in the north of Nigeria, in that arid part of the country, there were wide expressways constructed at great cost with the petrodollars which the delta belched forth. The injustice of it cried to the heavens. The fact that the victims of this injustice were too timid or ignorant to cry out against it was painful in the extreme. It was unacceptable. It had to be corrected at no matter what cost. To die fighting to right the wrong would be the greatest gift of life! Yes, the gift of life. And I felt better. What did a rough bus ride matter in the circumstances? It could be worse. May it be worse. The designers of the iniquitous system be ashamed. My spirit would not be broken. Never!

Day had begun to break. From the east, daylight streamed in with a fresh breeze, and soon the electric lights of the houses of Benin City came into view. We drove through the town and soon reached the Benin-Lagos road.

Driving past the University of Benin which lies on the road, I was reminded of a life which I would have liked to live: that of an academic. This was what I had always wanted in life. I had had to forgo it more than 25 years earlier when I was faced with the possible break-up of Nigeria during the civil war of 1967. At that time, the thought of the possible continued enslavement of the Ogoni people in nascent, if still-born, Biafra, had forced me to take personal risks and to identify myself with the Federal government.

I had not only given up my academic career; now, looking

back on those 25 years, I began to feel that I had also failed to end the enslavement of the Ogoni. Their condition had got marginally better, but the future looked bleak unless something was done urgently.

An hour or so out of Benin, the bus developed a flat tyre. It proved then that the spare tyre was not properly inflated and that we would need the services of a vulcaniser for both tyres. There was no vulcaniser in sight at that time of the morning. We all had to get down from the bus. And for the first time in ten hours or so, I had the opportunity to stretch my legs.

The man in the lounge suit, whom I now knew to be in charge of the party, was predictably furious with the driver. He could not understand how any police driver worth his salt would leave home without assuring himself that his spare tyre was in good condition. He nattered and grumbled on and on and on. To calm himself, he now produced a sheet of paper from his pocket and began to peruse it. I drew nearer to him and engaged him in conversation, while I peeped over his shoulder to see what his notes contained. I observed that it was a list of Ogoni youths who worked with me in the MOSOP. I was certainly not the only one slated for arrest. My brother, Owens, was also on the list. And he was the only one running a medical clinic in Bori. I bit my lips ruefully and took a little walk to steel my nerves, while I lit my pipe.

Within the hour the vulcaniser arrived and work was completed on the two tyres. The driver filled the tank of the vehicle from the jerry cans of petrol in the bus and soon we were on our way again to Lagos.

Chapter Two

WE arrived in Lagos at about 10.30 in the morning, having travelled for roughly 12 hours. We drove to the notorious Alagbon Close, to the offices of the Federal Investigation and Intelligence Bureau (FIIB). There, I was asked to sit behind the reception desk.

The reception area, like the rest of the complex, was extremely dirty. The walls were grimy with the marks of the years. The place had not been painted for ages. Nor, I thought, had the floor been swept in years. There was, as might be expected, a continuous flow of human traffic through the area and, seated on a wooden chair, I was a curious spectacle.

There was a telephone at the desk and I asked to be allowed to use it to contact my office. For a small consideration politely inferred, if not demanded, I was able to call Miss Joy Nunieh, a young Ogoni lawyer. I requested her to contact Dr Olu Onagoruwa, a well-known human rights lawyer, and inform him that I needed his services urgently. I also left word with my office to the effect that I was in Alagbon Close and in need of clothes, a transistor radio and food. This having been accomplished, I felt a little relieved.

Joy soon showed up to commiserate with me. Her office was close by and she arrived with sunshine smiles and best wishes. She had contacted Dr Onagoruwa's office and left word in his absence with one of his assistants. He had gone to court and she expected that once he returned to his chambers and got the message, he would be at Alagbon Close. Did I need anything? Yes, food. I had not eaten for 18 hours or so. Joy bade me goodbye.

At about three o'clock Dr Olu Onagoruwa's reassuring presence came into the reception area. I leapt upon my feet and welcomed him effusively. He was equally expansive and demanded to know what had happened. I narrated it all to him. After hearing me out, he asked to see the investigating police officer and was directed to one of the low buildings across the road.

As soon as Olu was gone, I was invited to another office beyond the reception area by one of the officers who had brought me from Port Harcourt. He demanded that I make another statement in relation to the 12 June presidential elections.

'But I already made a statement in Port Harcourt,' I asserted.

'That was in Port Harcourt. You are now in Lagos.'

'Isn't it the same police force throughout the country?'

'It is. You have to make a statement in Lagos. Please fill in the form.'

He was quite softly spoken, but there was a firmness in his voice. I was later to know him as Mr Inah, a close relation of my classmate at the University of Ibadan, Wilfred Inah, an Ogoja man, who had risen to become Secretary to the Government of Cross River State with headquarters at Calabar, Nigeria's first capital.

Without further ado, I made the required statement quickly and gave the form back to Mr Inah. He read it and asked that I elaborate further on what had happened to Dr Bennet Birabi, Senate Minority Leader, on Election Day. I asked if that was particularly important. He confirmed that it was.

Bennet was the son of possibly the most famous Ogoni man in modern times, T N Paul Birabi. Orphaned at the early age of three, he was looked after by his uncle and grandmother until he completed his primary education. At the time, I was working closely with the late Mr Edward Kobani, an educationist, in the Ogoni Divisional Union. He was president and I, secretary.

Love of and admiration for Birabi was the reason Ogoni Divisional Union decided to intervene in the education of young Bennet. Together, we decided that for all Paul Birabi meant to the Ogoni people, his two children would certainly get a proper education. Arrangement was made with the principal of Birabi Memorial Grammar School, who granted a concessional entry to the young boy.

Come the civil war, Bennet lost his grandmother in a refugee camp in the Igbo heartland. In 1969, as Commissioner for Education in Rivers State, I decided to send all the available senior secondary school boys in the state to the Baptist High School, Port Harcourt, as an emergency measure because of the lack of teachers and facilities. Bennet was one of the beneficiaries of the scheme.

He wrote to me, outlining his difficulties, and I wrote back asking him to consider himself a member of my household henceforth. At that time, I had in my house a large number of brothers and sisters and other young Ogoni whom I was assisting through school. There was not much around, but we all shared what was available as one family, without discrimination.

Bennet lived with us until he graduated from medical school, married and established a practice in Port Harcourt. I followed his career with very keen interest, but was somewhat disappointed when he threw in his lot in 1983 with the banned and subsequently disbanded National Party of Nigeria of the Second Republic. He seemed, like his father, destined for great things and even in the putrefaction of the Second Republic was able to win a seat in the House of Representatives and then to become a Federal Minister of State for 21 or so days.

Banned from politics after the military takeover at the end of 1983, he was available to partake in the activities of

MOSOP in 1990, but once the Babangida dictatorship lifted the ban, he joined the National Republican Convention and won a senatorial seat, becoming Senate Minority Leader.

Although thoroughly disenchanted with Babangida's quixotic political experiment, I was delighted with Bennet's position as it proved that Ogonis could rise to heights within the Nigerian system, weighted against them as it was. Unfortunately for Bennet, the system was as corrupt as it could be.

To return to my story, I did say all I knew about what had happened to the Senate Minority Leader and, with the answers to one or two questions added to the statement, signed it. Thereafter, I was asked to return to the reception desk.

Shortly afterwards, the sergeant at the desk was called away. Upon his return, he informed me that I was to go into the guardroom and instructed me to give him all my valuable property, including money, shoes, clutch-bag, watch and other things. I asked if I might keep my pen and some sheets of paper which were in my shirt pocket. He laughed. I believe that he knew well that in the guardroom I would find neither the time nor the opportunity to do any writing. I also asked him to allow me stay for a while, as I was expecting some clothes and particularly some underwear from my Lagos residence. I had been wearing the same clothes for two days and was feeling terribly uncomfortable. He agreed to let me be.

As I waited, word came that Dr Olu Onagoruwa wanted me at the office of the Assistant Commissioner of Police, to which he had gone earlier. I repaired there and met Olu with Assistant Commissioner of Police Kenneth Ogbeifun, the man in the lounge suit who had brought me from Port Harcourt. He appeared to be in charge of the team investigating my case.

Olu informed me that he had spoken with Mr Ogbeifun and that it appeared that he had not received specific instructions from his superiors as to what to do with me. I would have to stay in police custody for now, but he would file a case against my arrest the next day.

'I have been asked to go into the guardroom,' I informed them. 'I've heard terrible stories as to what goes on in there. Can anything be done to save me the agony?'

Olu pleaded with Mr Ogbeifun to give me what special consideration he could offer. The latter apologised that he had failed to do so in the first instance. He then took me to the reception desk and informed the sergeant on duty that I was not to go into the guardroom for the night but was to remain at the reception desk.

Olu stood chatting with me for a while. While we were thus, one of the detainees, a journalist from *News Magazine* who knew both Olu and me well, came in from the guardroom beyond. He apparently had been a guest. He was in the special uniform which, I believe, all those in police custody have to wear. Behind him was another young man in similar attire whom he introduced to us simply as 'The President'.

I was later to come close to the system whereby suspects in police custody ordered their lives in a special hierarchical order, assuming titles and responsibility over the lives of inmates. 'The President' was the boss of all the prisoners and he had responsibility of maintaining law and order in the guardroom! Quite a world of its own, and I was aware of it. Festus Iyayi, an award-winning Nigerian novelist, had been held in custody for a month in 1987 or thereabouts and had written about it in a Nigerian magazine. He had not been told what crime he had committed nor did his colleagues and employers know that he had been held.

Olu Onagoruwa soon left. Thanks to the order made by Kenneth Ogbeifun, I wasn't dumped into the guardroom, but the prospect of spending the night at the reception desk wasn't pleasant either. It was an open area, without doors and windows. Mosquitoes would make mincemeat of my body.

Joy Nunieh soon arrived, with a dish of rice and chicken, beer and ice-cold water. I was told that I couldn't have beer while in police custody and that I was to have my meal right there in the reception hall. I was hesitant so to do and asked if there was another room where I could have a measure of privacy.

The desk sergeant offered me a place in a low wooden building which must have been thought of as temporary when it was constructed. The building had since become permanent and now held a number of offices. The particular office into which I was led was most dreadful. Cobwebby, dusty, unswept, with broken cupboards and grimy desks lying in thorough disorder, I would rather not have had my meal there. But when I remembered that I had no alternative, I steeled myself and even convinced myself that it was as comfortable as the dining room in the Waldorf Astoria of New York City.

I hadn't had a meal for almost 48 hours. I washed it down with water and chattered at some length with Joy before she finally bade me goodbye. It was getting on for seven o'clock. She would see me the following day, she said.

Soon after she left, my young friend, Hauwa, arrived with a bag containing some clothes, underwear, transistor radio, books, including my first novel, *Sozaboy*. Shortly afterwards, my brother, Owens, turned up in the company of my youngest brother, Letam, a captain in the Nigerian army who had just completed his law studies at the University of Lagos. The presence of my brothers and Hauwa was comforting and my mind was taken off my ordeal. It was particularly nice of Owens to fly in from Port Harcourt, bringing with him my briefcase and a shoulder bag in which I often lodged the papers which my briefcase couldn't hold. Finally, Dr Broderick Ineneji, a civil rights lawyer and newly acquired friend, arrived. A highly experienced man who had worked for a long time in Britain and completed a doctoral thesis on ethnic minority problems, he was witty and engaging. Talking with him was quite a treat, and we had a bellyful of laughs; so much so, that we didn't notice the heavy rain which came down that night.

When the rain eventually stopped, they all bade me goodnight and I was left along to find some sleep in the only cushion chair in the room. It was well past 1.30 in the morning.

No, I couldn't sleep that night. The stuffy room, the mosquitoes singing about my ears, the thought of what the next day would bring, and worries about the Ogoni people kept me wide awake. Owens had told me of the events which had followed my departure from Port Harcourt the previous night, and I worried that, in my absence, the violence which I feared most might erupt. I prayed that this should not be, as I was more than anxious to keep the struggle at a non-violent level.

Had I known that earlier that day the Ogoni people, provoked by the treatment I had received, poured on to the streets of Bori to demonstrate their anger, and that some hoodlums had seized the opportunity to molest other citizens, I would have had a more troubled night.

As it was, I passed the night in doubt. I was not depressed only apprehensive.

Chapter Three

THE dawning day met me in a state of preparedness for uncertainty. The real problem was how to perform my ablutions. There wasn't a toilet in sight. I finally decided to ask the sergeant at the reception desk, who chortled ominously. A lavatory appeared to be a luxury in those parts. He did offer to show me one, asking me, however, to wait while he found water which I would use to flush the hallowed place.

To cut a long story short, I did manage to find some peace with the aid of the fumes from my pipe. Isn't it amazing what service this pipe often renders me?

I returned to my place in the office to tune in to the radio. I was listening to the BBC news at seven o'clock when Mr Inah came in. He asked me to follow him. I took up my bag and walked out. At the reception desk, I overheard him telling one of his subordinates to book him out as having travelled to Port Harcourt. I assumed then that I would be returning there with him. Fearful of another road journey back to Port Harcourt, I asked if we would be flying.

'No,' came the prompt reply.

'Listen,' I pleaded, 'another road journey to Port Harcourt from Lagos will virtually kill me. I haven't travelled that much by road in a long time. Besides, I'm not in the best of health. I'm prepared to pay the air fare for everyone so that we fly to Port Harcourt.'

'You can tell the Assistant Commissioner so when you see him.'

'Is he travelling with us?'

'Yes. We're going to his house now to collect him.'

Outside, the J5 Peugeot bus in which we had travelled the previous day was waiting. This time, there were none of the armed guards, which was some relief. Maybe I was no longer considered a dangerous criminal. The only other occupants of the bus were the driver and the third investigating police officer, the man in a kaftan who had sat next to me on our journey out of Port Harcourt.

We drove out of Ikoyi through the Third Mainland Bridge towards Ikeja. The bridge connects Lagos Island and Ikoyi to the mainland of Lagos and is one of the measures taken to ease traffic flow in the Lagos metropolis. The population of Lagos had exploded once oil money from the Delta had been cornered by the nation's rulers and transferred to Lagos from hapless communities like the Ogoni and the Ijaws who were too few to defend their inheritance. Most of that money was expended from and in Lagos, and it was to the latter city that the Dick Whittingtons and other carpetbaggers of Nigeria went to seek their fortune. Most of the money was also spent on foreign luxuries like cars, and soon the few roads in the city were clogged with cars, rendering movement well-nigh impossible. Overhead bridges became the norm in the city. These did not help much either, and so more bridges, such as the Third Mainland Bridge, had to be built. It had just opened to traffic and was predictably named after the dictator Babangida, who sat on the Nigerian throne at the time. Nor did it succeed in easing traffic.

That morning the bridge was as congested as ever, but since we were moving against the traffic, we had a very smooth journey. We stopped to buy newspapers and I observed that my arrest two days earlier was in the news.

We drove into the government residential area in Ikeja towards Mr Ogbeifun's residence. I noted ruefully how overgrown with weeds the area had become. The road was all potholes. I recalled my early days in Lagos while I was at the University of Ibadan in the years shortly after independence.

27

The area had been spick and span. Now it was virtually derelict. The houses occupied by civil servants were, of course, more run-down than others. The overall look of Ikeja was of general decline. And that was in spite of the huge amount of oil money transferred from the Niger River Delta to Lagos.

Mr Kenneth Ogbeifun was waiting for us when we arrived. He clambered into the bus after the morning's greetings. I immediately offered to fly all of us by air to Port Harcourt. Mr Ogbeifun said it was not possible. We had to pick up some other Ogoni detainees in Enugu or thereabouts. Could we then fly to Enugu? No, with finality. I resigned myself to another long road journey.

And who were those other Ogoni detainees? If I remembered correctly, only Mr N G Dube, a member of the Steering Committee of MOSOP had been held in Port Harcourt, and the information I had the morning of my arrest was that he had been released on bail. Mr Ogbeifun was not forthcoming on the matter and I decided not to press him further.

The journey that day was not very eventful. Mr Ogbeifun and his subordinates were quite relaxed and I engaged the former in a lively discussion on Nigerian politics. Of course, Mr Ogbeifun was very well informed and very engaging in his analysis of the subjects we discussed. He spoke English with an Edo (Benin) accent, and tended to sound cantankerous, but had quiet a sense of humour beneath his outwardly hard mien. I found him very interesting.

When I began to whine about breakfast, Mr Ogbeifun stopped the vehicle beside a roadside stall, where he bought me corn and coconut. At the next station petrol station, I bought bananas and groundnut from some hawkers and feasted on them. Yes, it was a feast. When you are on your way to becoming a beast, courtesy of the Nigerian security system, a wretched meal becomes a feast. It is part of the dehumanisation process.

At about one o'clock we arrived in Benin and I insisted on having lunch in a proper restaurant. I had been warned not to expect my captors to feed me. On such journeys they had to spend their own money and ask for reimbursement later. Such reimbursement often didn't appear. If it did, it could be a very long time coming.

The restaurant of the Palm Royal Motel was full when I entered and a few people recognised me. One diner decided to share my table with me.

'I thought you were in detention?' he asked.

'So I am.'

'Why are you in Benin?'

'I'm travelling under police escort from Lagos to Port Harcourt.' I nodded in the direction of the police officer in mufti who sat at a point where he could see me clearly. 'He is guarding me.' I said.

'But you were supposed to have been arrested in Port Harcourt two days or so ago.'

'So I was. And then I was taken to Lagos and now I'm going back to Port Harcourt.'

He digested my words with his meal. I think he found it difficult taking in all I had said.

'What are you being arrested for?'

'Election offences.'

'They should set you free soon.'

'Why?' I asked.

'CNN just announced the nullification of the election results.'

'You don't say!' I cried.

'It's true,' he said matter-of-factly. 'And all actions taken in regard of the elections are declared null and void.'

That put a new construction on my case. If, indeed, I was being held on an election offence, the nullification of the election negated the basis of my arrest. I ate the rest of my meal in silence.

I returned to the bus, to the waiting arms of Mr Obgeifun and his men, and drove to the centre of Benin, where my captors had their lunch.

As we drove out of Benin towards Onitsha, I informed my captors of the nullification of the elections and asked them banteringly if they hadn't wasted their labour and government funds holding me the way they had.

We discussed the nullification of the election exhaustively. Mr Ogbeifun, a history graduate of the University of Ibadan, was impressive in his analysis. The only thing he wouldn't be drawn on was its effect on my detention and what he would do in the circumstances.

After we crossed the Onitsha Bridge, I came to know that we were headed for Awka, although I didn't know what Mr Ogbeifun would be doing there. We arrived at about six o'clock in the evening and spent quite some time there while Mr Ogbeifun held discussions with his colleague. The driver had told me that he thought we would be spending the night. When he finally emerged, he gave orders that we were to move on.

'Where are we going?' I asked, and drew a blank.

I insisted.

'When we get there you will know,' Mr Ogbeifun answered unhelpfully.

In his discussion with his assistant, Mr Inah, it became clear that certain formalities had to be observed in order to make possible what they were going to do next.

This was of some interest to me. It occurred to me that after my seizure on the expressway in Port Harcourt I had been taken to the SSS office and had then been formally transferred to the SIIB in Port Harcourt. They, in turn, had formally transferred me to the FIIB in Lagos. This must have explained the busy human traffic in the office of the Assistant Commissioner of Police in Port Harcourt. The way they set about it, you might have thought they were engaged in legalities. I could only conclude that they were covering their tracks, just in case anything went wrong and they became accountable. All that formality was nothing but self-deception and utter waste!

We arrived at Abagana Police Station about 15 miles from Awka just past seven o'clock. A few minutes later, Mr N G

Dube and one other joined me in the bus. I was really delighted to see Mr Dube. He was his normal cheerful self. There was a lot to talk about but I didn't want to just yet. I asked about the other gentleman. He introduced himself as Mr Kabari Nwiee, Executive Officer with the Rivers State Schools Board. He was Chairman of the National Council of Ogoni People (NYCOP) in the village of Opuoko, in the eastern part of Ogoni.

It was utterly dark. A light rain had begun to fall and I was worried that I didn't exactly know where we were going. Could we possibly be heading for Port Harcourt? I must have dozed off for some time. When I opened my eyes, we were close to Owerri. And I was rather relieved when the bus turned off the Onitsha – Port Harcourt road in the direction of Owerri township. We subsequently drove into headquarters of the Imo State Police Command, Owerri. The time was 10 o'clock. The rain was pouring down now in earnest.

We waited an interminably long time as Mr Ogbeifun went into a long discussion with a tall, broad-shouldered senior police officer that desultory night. When he was done, he ordered us to get down from the bus with all our luggage. We obeyed his instruction. Then he led us to the reception desk where a police sergeant was on duty.

The reception area was the entrance to a long, two-storey building with rooms on both sides. Immediately to the right as you entered the building was a staircase leading to the upper floor. The ground floor had rooms for investigating police officers or, possibly, sergeants. From one of the rooms on the right came intermittent howls. I was to learn that this was the guardroom for suspects held in police custody.

We were led into a room next to the guardroom. There was no light in it, the only available light coming from a beam which fell from the fluorescent tube in the corridor. There was no door, the only door having fallen off its hinges. It was laid against the wall, and could be used to cover the opening in order to have some privacy. There were a few tables and chairs in the room. One particular chair was tied with a string to a table. Opposite the room was a bathroom from which came the stinking odour of human waste. This was to be our abode.

I took a look around and felt like throwing up. I placed my bag on one of the tables near what passed for a window giving out on to the courtyard. The smell of human waste came from that direction also. Much later, after I had been in Port Harcourt Prison, I realised that the smell was of the urine of the suspects in the guardroom who, at night, passed their urine into bottles and poured it through a chink in the wall to the ground outside.

Mr Ogbeifun was still with us, and I immediately complained about the conditions.

'I've done you a favour,' he replied stiffly. 'Would you rather be in the guardroom? That's where you should be. I've used my influence to secure you this special place. You should be thanking me, not complaining.'

I took counsel with myself and decided that the best I could expect from Mr Ogbeifun was that he contact my office in Port Harcourt so they would send me some money and make arrangements for food. He agreed to oblige me, bade us goodnight and disappeared into the darkness, it was about midnight.

Our quarters were a great improvement on what my fellow detainees were used to. Both Dube and Nwiee had been arrested in Port Harcourt, days before me, and had received the full treatment normally given to those in police custody. They had been thrown into the guardroom at the Central Police Station in Port Harcourt. There, they met hardened criminals and petty thieves who held court and charged newcomers specific fees. If you had no money, you were subjected to brutality and condemned to stand up all night to fan the guardroom bosses with old newspapers. If you had money, you might be allowed to stay outside the toilet room in which some of the inmates were forced to sleep, so cramped was the available space.

Of course, there was no food. Inmates had to depend on

food sent by their families. And whenever such food was sent, it had to be shared with the inmates, the bosses having the greater share thereof. Beatings were common in the guardroom and both Dube and Nwiee suffered a lot of indignities during their three-day stay there.

On the fourth day, both were ordered to sign a release paper. But instead of being set free, they were bundled into a Peugeot pick-up van and driven to the police station at Awka in Anambra State. There, late at night, they were thrown into a cell worse than they had had at Port Harcourt and infinitely more dehumanising. It was more cramped and the inmates more vicious. Worse, they had no money to give the cell bosses and so had to endure the worst beatings.

They were subsequently moved to nearby Aguata, where they found the cell full to busting. So, happy to have escaped the brutality of the cell bosses, they were content with the accommodation we now found. Tired to the teeth, they found an old mattress in the office and laid it on the hard floor. They then lay down and slept rather soundly, I thought.

I have spent some terrible nights in my life. But that night of Wednesday, 23 June 1993, must rank as one of the very worst in all of my experience. Without light in the room, with the stench from the window next to me, the howls of the inmates of the guardroom next door, and the turmoil in my soul, I considered myself as being as close to hell as possible. I turned to every conceivable station on my transistor radio and gathered every scrap of news I could get. And I prayed for daybreak, as my soul sang:

Prison Song
Bedbugs, fleas and insects
The Howl of deranged suspects
The dark night bisect
Rudely breaking my nightmare
I'm reminded of this crude place
Shared with unusual inmates

Strangely enough, and most uncharacteristically, I didn't give much thought to the nullification of the election on whose pretext I was being held. I had come to the conclusion long before then that nothing Babangida – the conman and dictator of Nigeria – did would surprise me. I considered him capable of just about anything. And yet I did feel that the nullification would become a significant turning point in the history of Nigeria.

When day finally broke, the first man I saw greeting me through the broken panes of the window was an Ogoni police constable who happened to be serving in Owerri. He was in mufti, being off-duty. Somehow, he had heard of our being at the station and had come calling. I gave him some money and the Port Harcourt telephone number of my assistant and friend, Apollos Onwuasoaku. He was to tell the latter that I was in Owerri, and ask that he please make arrangements for meals and to send me some money. He returned to confirm that he had been able to deliver the message by telephone. This was a welcome surprise because telephones do not normally work in Nigeria. I thanked him profusely.

Daylight brought into full view the dilapidated and miserable condition of our abode. The room in which we had passed the night had a number of lockers in which the policemen and officers stored their uniforms. They came to work in mufti and changed into their uniforms upon arrival. It also had 'exhibits' for cases which might never be heard: a 10-year-old dusty carpet, a broken-down fan and, of course, the old mattress on which files and sheets of paper piled up in one corner.

The office was like some sort of market. It was the SIIB and there was no shortage of people who had come to sort out one thing or another. For all those who wished to deal with investigating police officers, a 'waiting room' was created in an open-sided corrugated-iron shed outside the courtyard. Naturally, those waiting to transact 'business' had to be fed, so hawkers milled around the shed and there was quite some noise just next to the window where I had installed myself.

Earlier that morning the inmates of the guardroom had let forth a great howl, which I was to learn was their way of singing. The song, I was told, went something like 'Praise God, hallelujah! Praise God, amen!' The two lines were repeated over and over *ad nauseam*. This wild cacophony almost drove me round the bend that day when I first heard it.

The day dragged on interminably. Food was not forthcoming from the police, of course, and I had to provide for Dube and Nwiee. Towards evening, my staff arrived and with them my friend Mina, who brought me some food. At about the same moment Dr Garrick Leton and my cousin, Simeon Idemyor, came calling. They were shocked by the sight of our abode. We chatted for a while and they left with a promise to do something about our surroundings. Simeon had been in the Police Service Commission many years back and knew a number of the most senior officers. He hoped that he would be able to do something to make the Assistant Inspector General of Police responsible for the area offer us fair treatment.

The next day, Thursday 24 June, we continue to share the cell with police officers, and the noise and stench are quite unbearable. Towards late evening, a fine man, Assistant Commissioner of Police Innocent Ilozuoke, comes into the cell and officially welcomes us as his guests. I complain about the conditions, particularly the absence of light. There is not much he can do, I perceive, and let him be.

The night is an absolute disaster. Mosquitoes and the sounds from the overcrowded guardroom next door as well as the stench from the toilet and the human waste outside the paneless window, conjoin to aggravate my misery. When food arrives from Port Harcourt about 100 kilometres away, I shove it aside. I don't sleep all night. I sit by the table, tuning in to the radio. I am relieved, though, to find Dube and Nwiee sleeping soundly.

Early on Friday I follow the routine of the men in police custody with keen interest. There is the usual movement as they file out to perform their morning ablutions. I notice that there is a very young boy among them. He cannot, surely, be more than 12 years old. And that worried me beyond telling. What sort of effect is his situation going to have on his psyche? Why should he be held in police custody with adults? And when they get back to the cell and begin chanting their ghoulish song, 'Praise God, hallelujah!' I do not hear the wild cacophony; it is the young boy I see. And he is to assail my sensibilities all day.

Meanwhile, I notice that my health is deteriorating. At about 10 o'clock, I demand of Assistant Commissioner Ilozuoke to see a doctor who turns up at about 3.00 pm. He examines me, Dube and Nwiee and writes a prescription which he hands over to us. What are we expected to do with the prescription, we ask? We have no money and can buy no medicine. He leaves with a message that I need to see the cardiologist who has been managing me.

By now I have had enough of police brutality. I storm into the office of Mr Ilozuoke's assistant, a Mr Chime. On his table is a copy of Machiavelli's *The Prince* and also of Achebe's *Arrow of God*. I surmise quickly that he is either a reader or a mature student, most police officers being encouraged to take degrees in law if they do not already possess one. He is probably a man I can challenge.

I launch into a diatribe of the black man's inhumanity to his own kind, the trait responsible for the retardation of all blacks. It is inconceivable, I assert, that a man of my age can be subjected to the terrible indignities that have been meted out to me merely on suspicion, and which I feel sure cannot be sustained in a court of law. In any case, even if I were on death row, I would be entitled to my favourite meal. I resent being starved to death, I declare, and being asked to buy my medicine. And there is no reason why I should be kept in a room without light, a bed or toilet facilities.

It works. Apologies, apologies. We have been dumped on the Imo State Command by the FIIB without preparation or instruction. He will exert himself on our behalf. Did I mind

36

giving him an hour or so to hold discussions? He would get back to me.

A short while later, when Dr Leton and my cousin Simeon came again to see me, Mr Ilozuoke provided his personal funds, I later find out, to buy us food. He also ordered that we should be moved upstairs to his waiting room where conditions were marginally better. The stench was less, there was a fan, and although there was no bulb in the electrical connection on the ceiling, there were two dirty settees on which we could stretch. The Senior Police Officers' toilet is made available to us, thank God!

I arranged to have the toilet and waiting room cleared of cobwebs and other detritus, the floor was swabbed and we could now live somewhat like human beings. The two-seater settee was useful. My famed shortness of frame meant that I could sleep on the settee.

Mr Idoko later turned up with some medicine, the cheapest available, no doubt, and I was assured of some relief from a running stomach, seven boils on my left posterior, and my swollen feet. Not quite. The medicines were not efficacious – they may well have been out of date! But mercifully, my brother Owens arrived the next day and after discussions with the doctor offered me something more potent which gave me faster relief. Owens spent a lot of time with us, day after day, trying to ensure that my health was properly taken care of and that I was moved to a hospital or clinic as soon as possible.

On Saturday, Sunday and Monday, we had to beg for the single meal a day which was offered. There was still no news of our captors and our hosts kept reminding us that we are 'in transit' and therefore not their responsibility.

Meanwhile, the news from Ogoni was of youths protesting against my detention. I sent notes through Dr Leton and Barry Kumbe, the young lawyer from Mr Ledum Mitee's chambers, advising that I was alive and well and warning against the destruction of property. The note worked, I was later informed.

At the national level, citizens were responding to the humiliating insult which was the cancellation of the election. But leaderless or thoroughly misled, they did not develop a proper response to the situation. All were hurt but no-one appeared to know what to do. It is through preying on the non-mobilisation of the masses and the greed of the élite that Babangida has been able to assault the people of Nigeria and reduce them to intolerable levels of existence, dissipating all national assets in the process and plunging the nation deeper into debt. I felt sad that I couldn't contribute to this drama but had to watch it from the sidelines in illegal detention in a miserable cell.

Chapter Four

THE days and nights passed slowly, especially considering the frenetic pace of activity to which I was accustomed. Travelling constantly between Port Harcourt and Lagos and then Europe, I never had a dull moment. And there was always something new to do in each place I got to, all my efforts being bent to the improvement of the life of the Ogoni people and, by implication, the ethnic minorities and indigenous people of Nigeria, of Africa.

Now as I lay idle in an illegal detention, my thoughts went over my endeavours in this regard through the years.

My worry about the Ogoni has been an article of faith, conceived of in primary school, nurtured through secondary school, actualised in the Nigerian civil war in 1967-70 and during my tenure as a member of the Rivers State Executive Council, 1968-73.

My first thoughts on the matter were published in my pamphlet *The Ogoni Nationality Today and Tomorrow* issued in April 1969 in the throes of the civil war. It was essentially a young man's work, but it came straight from the heart. I had been a young graduate assistant at the University of Nigeria, Nsukka, when the civil war broke out. That war was mostly about the control of the oil resources of the Ogoni and other ethnic groups in the Niger River Delta.

By the end of 1967, the Federal forces were successful and they advanced into my Ogoni homeland. Appointed as a

Commissioner (Minister) in a fully fledged Rivers State Cabinet at the end of 1968, I worked officially to rehabilitate the Ogoni and other ethnic groups who had been the main victims of the war.

Trudging over the 100 rural villages in which the Ogoni lived, I was able to see for myself what the Ogoni as a people, needed. I worked tirelessly to bring them education and hope. But, even more importantly, I could see that what they required most was the formation of a mass organisation to press for their rights.

When the Biafran rebellion collapsed, many were forced to return to Ogoni and to Rivers State, of which Ogoni had become part following the break-up of former Eastern Nigeria into states. It fell to my lot to rehabilitate the returning Ogoni, and I did so without worrying about what role each had played in the Biafran débâcle.

I tried to reconcile one to each and each to the other and, when I judged it right, tried to set up a formalised structure in the Ogoni Development Association (ODA). Uniting the Ogoni masses, however, proved an easier task than associating a handful of graduates with my vision for the Ogoni. In the pamphlet *The Ogoni Nationality Today and Tomorrow* I had written, after tracing our communal failure to unite in the past, as follows:

We do ask that the disgrace from the past be our armour against the future. We must each of us immediately resolve not to repeat the mistakes of the past. We have now been given an opportunity to reassert ourselves side by side with all other nationalities in the Nigerian federation. We cannot let this opportunity slip past us. If we do, posterity shall not forgive us, and we shall disappear as a people from the face of the earth. This must not happen.

The spirit of self-sacrifice which moved Birabi is still alive in our nationality today. The men who think as he did are not lacking. The present crisis will have served to bring such men to the fore. They will provide enlightened and dynamic

40

leadership; they will, with active support, ensure that our nationality regains its lost dignity and honour, and transform our land for the betterment of our peoples. It is incumbent on us to entrust the future of our land to responsible persons who know what is going on in the world around them, and who will not succumb to petty inducements. This is important.

The Rivers State has been created, and a new Nigeria born. But we must remember that no matter the system of government, unless a people take their destiny into their own hands, no improvement will come to them. We cannot afford then to be complacent. We must begin immediately to organise ourselves enthusiastically for the difficult and turbulent days ahead. To start all over again is not going to be easy; the task will be made even more difficult by the uncertainty of the times and the hostility of some of our neighbours who have vowed to keep us as slaves for all time. But we must now bend to the labour. There is a great deal to be done and we must do it quickly and efficiently.

We reiterate that the task will not be easy. We shall be starting from a manifestly weak position. At the moment, the number of our people in the junior and senior cadre of the Federal public service and the corporations can be counted on the fingers of one hand. So also the number in the police and armed forces. Our children are largely out of school and university, many families have lost their breadwinners and our economy has collapsed completely. Our position is certainly not enviable, not even by comparison with other nationalities in the Rivers State. But the measure of our success will be the way, manner and time in which we turn this position of weakness into strength. It is not an impossible task, and we urge that the sufferings of the past year should not dishearten our young men and women. We stand convinced that we shall rise.

We shall appeal to the Federal military government, or whatever government succeeds it, to continue to show concern for small nationalities such as ours – especially in constitution-making; that it takes strong cognisance of our desires with regard to the companies prospecting or operating on our soil.

Our wish is that the Rivers State government so orders affairs in the state that all its component nationalities share in the prosperity and dignity which the state is expected to bring to the Rivers people as a whole. We must show that we have learnt from the mistakes of the past; and if there is a lesson to be learnt, it is that no group, however weak or small, can be taken for granted...

Looking back on these words now, I realise how pious my hopes were, and how much they failed. The Rivers State did not prove to be any better than the Eastern Region in reconciling the interest of its component ethnic groups. There was the usual bickering, the drive for supremacy on the part of the more numerous and the more powerful, and the Ogoni, unable to take care of their own interests, fell behind the others.

The Federal government, for its part, took on a unitary colour, thanks to the ruling military. In that unitarism, the resources of the Ogoni and other ethnic minorities in the Niger River Delta could be more easily purloined while paying lip-service to Nigerian federalism and unity.

The Nigerian constitution which emerged offered a stronger central government and left the ethnic minorities totally unprotected in terms of their economic resources and their culture. For instance, it vested the entire mineral resources in the country in parliament to share as it pleased. In a situation where the ethnic minorities provided most of the mineral resources (oil) and yet were a minority in parliament, and where oil was the be-all and end-all of Nigerian politics and the economy, as well as the central focus of all budgetary ambitions, there was no way the ethnic minorities, including the Ogoni, could protect their great inheritance. Thus, by 1980 the Federal government had left the oil-bearing areas with only 1.5 per cent of the proceeds of oil production. Before the military seized power, the governments in the areas were entitled to at least 50 per cent of such proceeds, in addition to rent and royalties.

In March 1990, my book *On a Darkling Plain* was published. Although I wrote most of the book as soon as the civil war ended in 1979, it had taken some time to convince myself of the right moment to make it public. I used the opportunity of the launch to speak about the obligations of the country to the oil-bearing delta and to make certain pronouncements about the future of Nigeria:

A civil war is a very divisive event; writing about it cannot be easy, especially when one is seeking to present the truth and that truth has as many sides to it as there are protagonists and interests. A civil war in a country with as many ethnic groups, religious sects, social classes and conflicts as Nigeria has serious repercussions for individuals, families and communities. Writing about it is equivalent to walking a minefield.

In spite of my hesitations about all that surrounded the last civil war, I wish to pay tribute to the men and women on both sides who fought against injustice, against hypocrisy and humbug as they saw it. We must ensure that those who died fighting, shall not have died in vain.

Many of those who participated in the war in one form or the other and survived it will readily agree that the country we fought for is not the country we have today. There is still more fighting to be done, in the minds of Nigerians, and for the minds of Nigerians, if the country we dream of is to emerge.

I wish to draw attention to two broad areas which my story and my study of Nigerian society have highlighted: the ethnic question and oil.

The ethnic nature of Nigerian society is a real one. It cannot be prayed or wished away and those who try to do so,

43

at least in public, only have to turn to the example of the Soviet Union, Yugoslavia and Romania to disabuse their minds. I therefore suggest that the make-up of the country as a federation of 300 ethnic groups be taken into full account in formulating policies of governance. The present division of the country into a federation in which some ethnic groups are split into several states, whereas other ethnic groups are forced to remain together in a difficult, unitary system inimical to the federal culture of the country, is a recipe for dissension and future wars. Chief Awolowo put it most succinctly: 'Under a true Federal constitution, each group, however small, is entitled to the same treatment as any other group, however large. Opportunity must be afforded to each to evolve its own peculiar political institution. The present structure reinforces indigenous colonialism – a crude, harsh, unscientific and illogical system.'

Oil was very much at the centre of the war. The people who live on oil-bearing land were the main victims of the war. Twenty years after the war, the system of revenue allocation, the development of policies of successive Federal administrations and the insensitivity of the Nigerian élite have turned the delta and its environs into an ecological disaster and dehumanised its inhabitants. The notion that the oil-bearing areas can provide the revenue of the country and yet be denied a proper share of that revenue because it is perceived that the inhabitants of the area are few in number is unjust, immoral, unnatural and ungodly. Why should the people on oil-bearing land be tortured? Why are they entitled to 1.5 percent of their resources? Why has this money not been paid as and when due? Where is the interest the money has generated over the last 10 years? The peoples of Rivers and Bendel States, in particular, sit very heavy on the conscience of Nigeria.

The silence of Nigeria's social reformers, writers and legal men over this issue is deafening. Therefore, the affected peoples must immediately gird their loins and demand without equivocation their rightful patrimony. They must not be frightened by the enormity of the task, by the immorality of the present. History and world opinion are on their side.

I call upon the Babangida administration to extend its human rights dispensation, its social justice claims to the minorities throughout Nigeria and, particularly, to the minorities of the delta and its environs. I call upon the administration to pay up all monies owed to the communities with interest and radically to increase the percentage of oil revenue payable to them.

I call upon the Nigerian élite to play fair by all Nigerian communities, to allow scientific methodology to replace sleight-of-hand as an instrument of social engineering and to show compassion to the less privileged of our society so that we can achieve a better Nigeria and hand over a meaningful legacy and a beautiful country to the future.

It was a controversial book. In a way, it was fortuitous that I was writing a column in the government-owned weekly *Sunday Times* at the time. I used the column, called 'Similia' to answer the critics of my new book, and to develop further the ideas which I had expressed in it.

The newspaper column widened my reading audience and spread my ideas to a considerable extent. Week after week, I made sure that the name Ogoni appeared before the eyes of readers. It was a television technique, designed to leave the name indelibly in their minds. Sometimes I would deliberately provoke readers or fly a kite in the acerbic and polemical column.

By the time the controversy over *The Darkling Plain* died down, I had stopped producing *Basi & Co*, a satirical comedy series that ran on Nigerian network television 1985-90, and the 'Similia' column was on its way out (it was becoming too anti-establishment and duly axed). The Ogoni question had begun increasingly to occupy my detailed attention.

45

I began the process of mobilising the Ogoni people by organising a seminar under the auspices of the newly formed Ogoni Central Union, of which I had been elected President. The best Ogoni brains presented papers on aspects of Ogoni life; culture and education, the disorganisation of the Ogoni, their traumatic existence, agriculture, the economy and women. The seminar conclusions pointed to the need for the Ogoni people to organise themselves better and to take responsibility for their political existence.

I canvassed the idea of forming a mass organisation with Kagote, a club for the Ogoni élite, and the Ogoni Klub, another club for young Ogoni professionals. I attended meeting after meeting with them and pressed my views hard all the time. I found a ready response.

When I proposed the signing of an Ogoni Bill of Rights under the auspices of the Ogoni Central Union, no one demurred. On 26 August 1990, we met at Bori, the headquarters of the Ogoni people.

Presented to the government and people of Nigeria
We, the people of Ogoni, numbering about 500,000, being a separate and distinct ethnic national within the Federal Republic of Nigeria, wish to draw the attention of the government and people of Nigeria to the undermentioned facts:

That the Ogoni people, before the advent of British colonialism, were not conquered or colonised by any other ethnic group in present-day Nigeria.

That British colonisation forced us into the administrative division of Opobo from 1908 to 1947.

That we protested against this forced union until the Ogoni Native Authority was created in 1947 and placed under the then Rivers Province.

That in 1951 we were forcibly included in the Eastern Region of Nigeria, where we suffered utter neglect.

That we protested against the neglect by voting against

the party in power in the region in 1957, and against the forced union by testimony, before the Willink Commission of Inquiry into Minority Fears in 1958.

That the protest led to the inclusion of our nationality in Rivers State in 1967, which state consists of several ethnic nationalities with differing cultures, languages and aspirations.

That oil was struck and produced in commercial quantities on our land in 1958.

That oil has been mined on our land since 1958 to this day by Shell Petroleum Development Company (Nigeria) Limited.

That in over 30 years of oil mining, the Ogoni nationality have provided the Nigerian nation with a total revenue estimated at over 40 billion naira, 30 billion dollars.

That in return for the above contribution, the Ogoni have received NOTHING.

That today, the Ogoni people have:

No representation whatsoever in ALL institutions of the Federal government of Nigeria.

No pipe-borne water.

No electricity.

No job opportunities for the citizens in Federal, state, public sector or private sector companies.

No social or economic project of the Federal government.

That the Ogoni languages of Gokana and Khana are undeveloped and are about to disappear, whereas other Nigerian languages are being forced on us.

That the ethnic politics of successive Federal and state governments are gradually pushing the Ogoni people to slavery and possible extinction.

That the Shell Petroleum Development Company of Nigeria Limited does not employ Ogoni people at a meaningful or any level at all, in defiance of the Federal government's regulations.

That search for oil has caused severe land and food

shortages in Ogoni, one of the most densely populated areas of Africa (average 1,500 per square mile; national average 300 per square mile).

That neglectful environment pollution laws and substandard inspection techniques of the Federal authorities have led to the complete degradation of the Ogoni environment turning our homeland into an ecological disaster.

That the Ogoni people lack education, health and other social facilities.

That it is intolerable that one of the richest areas of Nigeria should wallow in abject poverty and destitution.

That successive Federal administrations have trampled on every minority right enshrined in the Nigerian constitution to the detriment of the Ogoni and have, by administrative structuring and other noxious acts, transferred Ogoni wealth exclusively to other parts of the republic.

That the Ogoni people wish to manage their own affairs.

Now, therefore, while reaffirming our wish to remain a part of the Federal Republic of Nigeria, we make demand upon the Republic as follows:

That the Ogoni people be granted Political Autonomy to participate in the affairs of the Republic as a distinct and separate unit by whatever name called, provided that this autonomy guarantees the following:

- political control of Ogoni affairs by Ogoni people;
- the right to control the use of a fair proportion of Ogoni economic resources for Ogoni development;
- adequate and direct representation as of right in all Nigerian national institutions;
- the use and development of Ogoni languages in Ogoni territory;
- the full development of Ogoni culture;

- the right to religious freedom;
- the right to protect the Ogoni environment and ecology from further degradation.

We make the above demand in the knowledge that it does not deny any other ethnic group in the Nigerian Federation their rights and that it can only be conducive to peace, justice and fair play and hence stability and progress of the Nigerian nation.

We demand these rights as equal members of the Nigerian Federation who contribute and have contributed to the growth of the Federation and have a right to expect full returns from that Federation.

As adopted by general acclaim of the Ogoni people on the 26th day of August, 1990 at Bori, Rivers State.

The document was despatched to Babangida's Armed Forces Ruling Council. The die had been cast.

By the end of the year, there was considerable excitement in Ogoni over the Ogoni Bill of Rights. I continued to press the case for non-violent struggle at every available forum. On 26 December 1990, I spoke to the Kagote Club at its annual luncheon:

I am sure that you all know the very serious circumstances in which Ogoni finds itself today. Never before in the history of our nationality have we been faced collectively by such terrible challenges. Never before has there been need for unity, unanimity and consensus.

Historically, the Ogoni people have always been fierce and independent. They have been known to 'display an exceptional achievement in their original, abstract masks'. As storytellers and in other forms of art the Ogoni are gifted and hold their own easily. The Ogoni have made contributions of the first order to modern African literature in English. And Ogoni was, before the advent of British

49

colonialism, a very orderly society.

The advent of British colonialism was to shatter Ogoni society and inflict on us a backwardness from which we are still struggling to escape. It was British colonialism which forced alien administrative structures on us and herded us into the domestic colonialism of Nigeria. Right from 1908 when Ogoni was administered as part of Opobo Division, through the creation of Rivers Province in 1947, Eastern Region in 1951 and Rivers State in 1967, the Ogoni people have struggled to resist colonialism and return to their much cherished autonomy and self-determination. I am encouraged to think that this heroic struggle by our people is beginning to see the light at the end of a very dark tunnel.

Some of you here have taken part in this struggle from the very early days. Most of you must be aware of the struggles in the 1930s through the 1950s of Birabi and others in the Ogoni Central Union and the Ogoni State Representative Assembly.

I have to state without equivocation that this struggle has been made doubly difficult by what I have characterised as the crude and harsh nature of Nigerian domestic colonialism, a colonialism which is cruel, unfeeling and monstrous. Its method has been an outrageous denial of rights, a usurpation of our economic resources, a dehumanisation which has sought to demoralise our people by characterising them as meek, obscure and foolish. If we have been able to achieve what we have in our dire circumstances, can anyone imagine what we would have done had we benefited from equal opportunities?

As a result of domestic colonialism, the Ogoni people have virtually lost pride in themselves and their ability, have voted for a multiplicity of parties in elections, have regarded themselves as perpetual clients of other ethnic groups and have come to think that there is nowhere else to go but down.

When you consider the census cheating, the

administrative malstructuring, the unfair revenue allocation formulations, the lack of protection of minority rights in the Nigerian constitution, we must regard it as something of a miracle that Ogoni still exists at all. Yes, we merely exist; barely exist. Most of our children are not at school, while those who have secured an education do not find jobs. Those who have jobs do not find promotion, as progress in Nigeria is not by merit but by preferment. Our languages are dying, our culture is disappearing. For a people who proved themselves as providers of food to those who live in the inhospitable delta, the fact we are buying food today is an absolute disgrace. Land is in very short supply in Ogoni and what is available is no longer enough to feed our teeming population. Where will our children live and farm 20 years hence? The Ogoni do not have the share in the economic life of Nigeria.

And all this is happening to a people whose home is one of the richest in Africa. Over the past 32 years Ogoni has offered Nigeria an estimated US 30 billion dollars and received nothing in return, except a blighted countryside, and atmosphere full of carbon dioxide, carbon monoxide and hydrocarbons; a land in which wildlife is unknown; a land of polluted streams and creeks, of rivers without fish; a land which is, in every sense of the term, an ecological disaster. This is not acceptable.

What to do? Hopeless as the situation is, bleak as the picture is, we can and must do something to save Ogoni. The responsibility is yours and mine, and we must all co-operate to redeem our nationality, to save our progeny.

As clearly enunciated in the Ogoni Bill of Rights presented to the government and people of Nigeria in October 1990, the only thing that will save the Ogoni people is the achievement of political autonomy accompanied by, among others, the right to use a fair proportion of Ogoni resources for the development of Ogoni – its education, health, agriculture and culture. This is the great task before us in this last decade of the twentieth century.

Some, looking at the enormity of the task, must ask 'Can we do it?' The answer, unequivocally, is, YES. For where there is a will, there is always a way. Ogoni must be saved.

We have taken the first important step in clearing our minds, in achieving unity of leadership, in projecting our case before Nigeria and, I must tell you, before some international organisations interested in the matter. The next task is to mobilise every Ogoni man, woman and child on the nature and necessity of our cause so that everyone knows and believes in that cause and holds it as a religion, refusing to be bullied or bribed therefrom. And finally we must begin to build action to transform our current advantages into political scores.

This is not, I repeat, NOT a call to violent action. We have a moral claim over Nigeria. This moral claim arises as much from the murder of 30,000 Ogoni people during the civil war by Ojukwu's followers as from the usurpation of US 30 billion dollars' worth of our oil and the destruction of our ecology amounting to the same sum. Our strength derives from this moral advantage, and that is what we have to press home.

You will, therefore, find that the Ogoni people have an agenda and everyone, as I have said, has a role in actualising that agenda. This is no time to feast and make merry like sheep being led unwittingly to the slaughterhouse. This is a time to think and act. Brothers and sisters, be courageous in asking for Ogoni rights. Morality, time and world opinion are on our side.

Wherever an Ogoni man or woman may be, he must not forget our agenda to save our nationality, our language, our culture, our heritage. Ogoni people must co-operate with one another, as individuals, as groups, because that is the only way we can survive. Wherever they may be, they must proclaim their Ogoniness, from the rooftops if possible. The

Ogoni are so far down the well that only by shouting loudly can they be heard by those on the surface of the soil.

In the ongoing political exercise, I think it is well to understand that, no matter which of the parties wins, no difference will be made to the generality of the Ogoni people. Both parties are built on fundaments inimical to Ogoni progress. Therefore, the Ogoni people and their politicians must not break their heads over which of the parties wins, can win, does not win, should win.

However, we must support the progression to democratic rule, as it is only through democratic action that we can re-establish our rights. The duty of the party politicians among us is to represent Ogoni, their constituencies; to push the Ogoni agenda within their parties. I believe that the Ogoni agenda is the only one that can save Nigeria from future destruction. This agenda postulates the equality of all ethnic groups, big or small, within the Nigerian federation as well as the evolution of proper, undiluted federalism in the nation. In this way, Nigerians will not be oppressed: their creative spirit will be freed and their productivity and self-reliance promoted. Cheating will end in the nation, corruption will be minimised and justice will prevail.

Not long after this, at a meeting in Bodo, in the residence of Edward Kobani, the name of the organisation, Movement for the Survival of the Ogoni People (MOSOP) was chosen.

At this time I still had all my balls in the air. I was about to end the television production of *Basi & Co,* and the 'Similia' column in the *Sunday Times* was also about to end. It had been a busy year. Apart from my usual routine, I was also able to visit the Soviet Union at the invitation of the African Institute of that country, and later in the year I was touring the United States.

The two visits were important in the development of the Ogoni cause, which had, at that time, become the greatest of my concerns. In the Soviet Union I was able to see the beginning of the death of a multi-ethnic state where the ethnic groups had been held together by force and violence. The rumbles of disintegration had already started.

The visit to the United States sharpened my awareness of the need to organise the Ogoni people to struggle for their environment. One visit to a group in Denver, Colorado, interested in the trees in the wilderness of the Colorado State, showed what could be done by an environment group to press demands on government and companies.

A bit of research and thinking of my childhood days showed me how conscious of their environment the Ogoni have always been and how far they went in an effort to protect it. I had always felt part of that consciousness myself. It is reflected in my pamphlet *The Ogoni Nationality Today and Tomorrow*, published during the Nigerian civil war in 1968:

'We refuse to accept that the only responsibility which Shell-BP owes our nation is the spoliation of our lands ... '

And in the lines of a poem I had written:

> The flares of Shell are flames of hell
> We bake beneath their light
> Nought for us save the blight
> Of cursed and neglect and cursed Shell.

I had also played a major role in attempting to get Shell to pay reparation to the Ogoni landlords after the blow-out on Shell's Bomu Oilwell 11 in 1971. What the trip did was to convince me that the environment would have to be a strong plank on which to base the burgeoning Movement for the Survival of the Ogoni People.

I returned to Nigeria knowing that my career as a business-man was effectively over, and so also my television production work. After my article 'The Coming War in the Delta', the 'Similia' column was axed, thus serving notice that my arguments for the Ogoni and the humiliation of the people of the oil-bearing areas of the delta were not acceptable to the

Babangida administration. Dr Ogunbiyi, my boss, was himself under pressure for not turning the newspaper into a megaphone of the government, and was soon dismissed unceremoniously, bringing to an end a very exciting period in the life of the *Daily Times* Group.

From that moment onwards, I dedicated myself in full to the Ogoni cause. I sorted out at the back of my mind the two facets of the case: the complete devastation of the environment by the oil companies prospecting for and mining oil in Ogoni, notably Shell and Chevron. And second, the political marginalisation and economic strangulation of the Ogoni, which was the responsibility of succeeding administrations in the country. And I began to cast about for ways of confronting both institutions.

The year 1991 marked my fiftieth on earth and I proposed to publish no less than eight books, seven of them mine. At the launch I made certain proposals on the Nigerian condition, it being my credo that literature in a critical situation such as Nigeria's cannot be divorced from politics. Indeed, literature must serve society by steeping itself in politics, by intervention, and writers must not merely write to amuse or to take a bemused, critical look at society. They must play an interventionist role. My experience has been that African governments can ignore writers, taking comfort in the fact that only few can read and write, and that those who read find little time for the luxury of literary consumption beyond the need to pass examinations based on set texts. Therefore, the writer must be *l'homme engagé*: the intellectual man of action.

He must take part in mass organisations. He must establish direct contact with the people and resort to the strength of African literature – oratory in the tongue. For the word is power and more powerful is it when expressed in common currency. That is why a writer who takes part in mass organisations will deliver his message more effectively than one who writes waiting for time to work its literary wonders. The only problem I see is that such a writer must strive to maintain his authenticity, which stands a chance of being corrupted by the demands of politics. A struggle will necessarily ensue, but that should conduce to make the writer even better. For we write best of the things we directly experience, better of what we hear, and well of what we imagine.

This is probably the reason why the best Nigerian writers have involved themselves actively in 'politics'. Wole Soyinka, Nigeria's Nobel Laureate, is an outstanding example. Even the normally placid and wise Chinua Achebe was forced to work within one of the political parties to buttress his call on all Nigerians to 'proselytise' for civilised values'. Chris Okigbo died fighting on the side of the Biafran secessionists. And Festus Iyayi has been involved in labour unions and recently in the Campaign for Democracy organisation. Which only goes to prove what I have said elsewhere: that in a situation as critical as Nigeria's, it is idle merely to sit by and watch or record goons and bumpkins run the nation aground and dehumanise the people.

This is not to say that I discount the value of those who only write, stand and wait. I am only reacting to my social situation, as every writer must. Accordingly, my speech at the launch was long on politics, short on literature:

Before the Curtain Falls

A writer is his cause. At 50, he may still dream dreams and see visions, but he must also venture into the truth. So today, I re-dedicate myself to what has always been my primary concern as a man and a writer: the development of stable, modern Nigeria which embraces civilised values; a Nigeria where no ethnic group or individual is oppressed; a democratic nation where minority rights are protected, education is a right, freedom of speech and association are guaranteed, and where merit and competence are held as beacons. Convinced that most Nigerians share this concern, I will stand for it at all times and in all places.

If there was ever any doubt that the Nigeria of our dreams is far away, the recent World Bank Report on Nigeria has put paid to such doubts. What we have today is the rump of a country, illiterate, lacking in moral fibre, financially bankrupt and tottering dangerously on the brink of disaster. This should shake us out of all complacency.

The great issues of today are the structure of the Federation, our environment, an economy laden with debts which we must pay and not merely reschedule to the detriment of our children, education and the future of our youth.

So long as the structure of the Federation is weak, so long shall we continue to stumble from military dictatorships to civilian chaos with the same result: anarchy. Nigeria is a federation of ethnic groups. Since 1966 the military have sought to turn this federation into a unitary system with the same dismal results. Historical forces at work in the world dictate that all multi-ethnic states become confederations of independent ethnic groups. The Soviet Union and Yugoslavia are cases in point. Nigeria cannot waltz in an opposite direction. Current attempts to do so, if not immediately reversed, could lead to the total collapse of the nation.

We must end immediately oppression of minority ethnic groups and free all Nigerians to express themselves and develop their cultures, their languages and their political systems, using their resources as best they may. The late Chief Obafemi Awolowo said so almost 50 years ago. The nation has degenerated by the same measure as we have failed to pay heed to his thoughts.

Oil pollution is a great menace to the Nigerian environment. I wish to warn that the harm being done to the environment of the Niger River Delta must be ameliorated by the oil companies which prospect for oil there; the degradation of the ecosystem must end and the dehumanisation of the inhabitants of the areas must cease and restitution be made for past wrong.

It has been said that the way to the future is the current transition programme, which is expected to lead to democratic civilian rule. This second attempt is basically no different from the 1979 experiment. And it is headed in a more disastrous direction. The transition has been described as a train, and is said to be on course. I disagree. The train is rusty and stands in the station; its route is strewn with danger, the passengers in the train are suffering and hungry, the large majority of passengers and their goods are not on board. I do not believe that in the space of one year we can peacefully hold six elections and a census. Besides, the constitution which is meant to usher in democracy is faulty: it does not protect minority rights, a basic requirement for democracy; it has been doctored by the military; the recent creation of new states and local governments has vitiated most of its tenets.

Over the past 30 years, a few military men have tried to dictate what course the nation should take. The result has been uniformly unedifying, as the military themselves have acknowledged recently. The look of a democratic Nigeria cannot, should not, be decided by military decree; it must be the collective decision of all Nigerians operating in a democratic context without coercion. The military are dedicated Nigerians but they should now honourably retire without equivocation from the political process, and take their proper place within the nation, so that Nigerians can resume the search for good government without fear of intimidation.

I am not by this bashing the military. No. Quite clearly, what we are faced with is a massive failure of vision and intellect on the part of the Nigerian élite – that failure which led to the easy enslavement of Africa, which has made Africans the playthings of other peoples and other races, which made African rulers persist in the slave trade long after Europe had tired of it.

Anyone who witnessed the killings, looting, and burning engineered during civilian rule in 1964 and 1965; anyone who witnessed the massive electoral fraud and the treasure looting of the civilians of 1979-83 that drove Nigeria into debt peonage and reduced all Nigerians into Sap-induced slavery, must tremble at the thought that this country is about to return to civilian rule.

Anyone who thinks that splitting Nigeria into 50 states and 600 local governments is about to solve the problems of ethnic oppression, competitive ethnicity, economic mismanagement, moral ineptitude and other evils is applying a simplistic solution to a complex problem.

Nigerians of the majority ethnic groups must ask themselves if they must mindlessly grind the minority ethnic groups to the dust, cheat and rob them openly, drive them into extinction, all in the name of what?

In 1958 it was obvious that the federating ethnic groups of Nigeria needed to establish the fundament of their co-operation. The British opined that if that were to be done, independence would have to be postponed. Nigerian leaders decided to have independence first and talk later. They only got to talk in 1966 after the several murders of political leaders and massacres of common people. But the Ad-hoc Conference of 1966 called by Gowon, (the leader of the Federalists) was scuttled by Ojukwu (the leader of the Biafrans), when the discussions did not appear to going in the direction the latter wanted. We plunged into civil war.

Many of the issues raised by Ojukwu which led to the civil war are as valid today as they were then. The untidy end of the war, the scampering of the ideologues of Biafra who have failed to sustain their arguments, greed for oil of the delta, and the impatience of the Nigerian military with philosophy have conjoined to stop Nigerians from seeking a rational solution to their collective dilemma.

Our ship of state is today sinking! A few are manipulating the system to their advantage, but our intellectuals, our women, our youth, the masses are being flushed down the drain. All our systems – educational, economic, health – are in a shambles. Yet we persist in our national obtuseness. Sycophancy and self-deceit lie to the public and try to convince us that all is well or will soon be so. No. As I say in *Basi & Co*, to be, we have to think.

The words of Descartes, *Cogito ergo sum*. Nigerians must think deeply. We must shun the simplistic solutions now being proffered.

I cast no blame on individuals or groups. I only want to mitigate that disaster which superficial thinking or even lack of thought has visited on Africa in the last 700 or so years. Nigeria deserves better than what we have now.

I therefore suggest that the elected representatives of all ethnic groups in Nigeria should gather at a National Conference to select an interim government consisting of 20 reputable Nigerian men and women, including retired judges of proven integrity, religious leaders, retired diplomats, intellectuals and elder statesmen from all parts of the country. The interim government will remain in office for one year while the National Conference discusses a more durable political structure and other extra-constitutional issues that will conduce to a more progressive, stable and democratic country.

I call upon all the minority ethnic groups in Nigeria to follow the example of the Ogoni people and demand their rights to political autonomy and freedom from Nigeria. In times past, such minority commitment has saved Nigeria. It can be so even now as the nation stands on the crossroads once again.

I also appeal to the Nigerian press to continue to stand courageously for a democratic Nigeria according to the wishes of all Nigerians, to crusade for social justice and for the rights and liberties of the oppressed masses, oppressed ethnic groups and the disadvantaged of our country. Else the curtain will fall.

Even as I wrote, edited and published the books, I continued to search for assistance in my major project of confronting the denigration of the Ogoni. I had met William Boyd, the celebrated British writer, in England at a seminar in Cambridge in 1988. Having read his book, *A Good Man in Africa*, I was delighted when he turned up to do a reading of his work in progress. I asked him why he had set the book in Ibadan.

'My father was a doctor at the University of Ibadan' he replied. And it all came together. I remember the Dr Boyd of our days in Ibadan University. A good, funny doctor he was, much beloved by students. He had a fund of stories about his reaction to their favourite illness: the clap. I introduced myself to William, and he recognised the author of *Sozaboy*, a book which he told me he had enjoyed very much. And from that moment there developed a friendship.

It was to William that I turned whenever I hit a brick wall in my solicitation on behalf of the Ogoni. On his advice, in 1991, I telephoned Greenpeace. 'We don't work in Africa,' was the chilling reply. When I called up Amnesty, I was asked, 'Is anyone dead? Is anyone in a jail?' And when I replied in the negative, I was told nothing could be done. Was I upset? The Ogoni people were being killed, all right – but in an unconventional way. Amnesty was only interested in conventional killings. And as to Greenpeace, why would it not show concern for Africa? For Ogoni? It did seem that the Ogoni were destined for extinction.

I returned from London, after that particular trip, in cavernous despair. The experience went into preparing an addendum to the Ogoni Bill of Rights, which was advertised in the Nigerian press in August 1991 as 'An Appeal to the International Community'.

In the Addendum, we noted that on 2 October 1990 we had addressed an Ogoni Bill of Rights to the President of the Federal Republic of Nigeria, General Ibrahim Babangida, and members of he Armed Forces Ruling Council. After a one-year wait, the President had been unable to grant us the audience which we sought in order to discuss the legitimate demands contained in this Bill of Rights. We noted too that the

Government of the Federal Republic of Nigeria had continued to decree measures and implement policies which further marginalised the Ogoni people, denying us political autonomy, our rights to our resources, to the development of our languages and culture, to adequate representation of right in all Nigerian national institutions and to the protection of our environment and ecology from further degradation.

'We cannot sit idly by while we are, as a people, dehumanised and slowly exterminated and driven to extinction, even as our rich resources are siphoned off to the exclusive comfort and improvement of other Nigerian communities, and the shareholders of multinational oil companies.

Now, therefore, while affirming our wish to remain a part of the Federal Republic of Nigeria, we hereby authorise the Movement for the Survival of the Ogoni People (MOSOP) to make representation, for as long as these injustices continue, to the United Nations Commission on Human Rights, the Commonwealth Secretariat, the African Commission on Human and People's Rights, the European Community and all international bodies which have a role to play in the preservation of our nationality.'

We repeated our demand for recognition of our political right to self-determination, economic rights to our resources, cultural rights to the development of our languages and culture, and social rights to education, health and adequate housing and to representation as of right in national institutions. We highlighted, in particular, the refusal of the Federal Republic of Nigeria to pay us oil royalties and mining rents amounting to an estimated US 20 billion dollars for petroleum mined from our soil for over 33 years.

We also stated clearly that the multi-national oil companies, namely Shell (Dutch/British) and Chevron (American) had severally and jointly devastated our environment and ecology, having flared gas in our villages for 33 years and caused oil spillages and blow-outs. They had dehumanised our people, denying them employment and those benefits which industrial organisations in Europe and America routinely contribute to their areas of operation. The Nigerian élite, meanwhile, (bureaucratic, military, industrial and academic) had turned a blind eye and a deaf ear to these acts of dehumanisation by the ethnic majority and had colluded with all the agents of destruction aimed at us.

'We cannot seek restitution in our courts of law in Nigeria, as the act of expropriation of our rights and resources has been institutionalised in the 1979 and 1989 constitutions of the Federal Republic of Nigeria, which constitutions were acts of a constituent assembly imposed by a military regime and do not, in any way, protect minority rights or bear resemblance to the tacit agreement made at Nigerian independence.'

The Addendum concluded with the declaration:

'That the Ogoni people abjure violence in their just struggle for their rights within the Federal Republic of Nigeria but will, through every lawful means, and for as long as necessary, fight for social justice and equity for themselves and their progeny, and in particular demand political autonomy as a distinct and separate unit within the Nigerian nation.'

Without the intervention of the international community, the government of the Federal Republic of Nigeria and the ethnic majority will continue these noxious policies until the Ogoni people are obliterated from the face of the earth.'

I did recognise that other groups were suffering the same fate as the Ogoni. To tackle the wider problem, we needed to establish organisations which would deal with the environmental and political problems of threatened peoples. And so

63

were born the Ethnic Minority Rights Organisation of Nigeria and the Nigerian Society for the Protection of the Environment, both of which later merged into the Ethnic Minority Rights Organisation of Africa (EMIROAF).

In October 1990, just before I went on my trip to the United States, youths in the Etche community of Rivers State, neighbours of the Ogoni, were protesting against the destructive actions of Shell in the area. As usual, they were visited with high-handed brutality by the authorities. About 80 people were brutally murdered and almost 500 houses razed to the ground. The news filtered through to England, where two filmmakers, Glen Ellis and Kay Bishop, were already examining the activities of Shell in the Developing World. That report brought them to Port Harcourt, and thus the Ogoni case came to be shown in the documentary film *The Heat of the Moment*, which was shown on Channel 4 in the United Kingdom in October 1992.

Glen and Kay promised to assist me in subsequent visits to the United Kingdom. And they were as good as their word. At my next visit, we went knocking on several doors: Friends of the Earth, Survival International, and others. Again, we drew a blank, but I was receiving a much valued education.

In June of 1992 I found myself on a sponsored trip to Germany to take part in a summer literature seminar at the University of Bayreuth. I asked to be permitted to visit Göttingen, to meet with a non-governmental organisation, the Association of Threatened Peoples of Germany. There, it was impressed on me that going to Geneva to participate in the United Nations Working Group on Indigenous Populations would be helpful. For one, I would be able to present the Ogoni case before a world audience, and for another, I would meet several non-governmental organisations interested in human rights.

And so to Geneva I went that summer of 1992. I had earlier been in contact with the Unrepresented Nations and Peoples Organisation (UNPO), which also sent an invitation to EMIROAF to come to Geneva, offering to hold workshops which would enable us to learn how to work with the United Nations.

The UNPO was a real find. The organisation had been set up two years earlier by a young Dutch lawyer, Michael van Walt van der Praag, the polyglot son of a Dutch diplomat who had represented the legal interests of the Dalai Lama. His contact with the Tibetan question led him to the conclusion that there were several peoples all over the world who needed to be heard, whose interests need to be represented in the international forums, and who needed to be guided to struggle non-violently for their rights. The organisation had grown rapidly and was already making an impact on peoples in the former Soviet Union, in Asia and even in Europe.

I learnt a lot from Michael about the ways of the United Nations and its Human Rights Commission, and he patiently guided me on this first contact with the UN. The great appeal of the UNPO for me was its insistence that its members forswear violence in their struggle for local autonomy, self-determination or independence.

UNPO had a small outfit based at The Hague and staffed almost entirely by volunteers who had more than the normal share of dedication. The organisation was later to play a very prominent role in the Ogoni struggle as indeed in other struggles, including in Abkhazia, Chechnya and Bougainville.

That summer, I made a representation to the Working Group on Indigenous Populations:

Ogoni territory lies on 404 square miles of the coastal terraces to the northeast of the Niger River Delta. Inhabited by 500,000 people, its population density of about 1,500 per square mile is among the highest in any rural area of the world and compares with the Nigerian national average of 300.

The Ogoni people have settled in this area as farmers and fishermen since remembered time and had established a well-organised social system before the British colonialist invaded them in 1901. Within 13 years, the British had destroyed the fabric of Ogoni society. British rule of the area was 'haphazard' and no treaties were signed with the Ogoni. By 1960, when colonial rule ended, the British had consigned the Ogoni willy-nilly to a new nation, Nigeria, consisting of 350 or so other peoples previously held together by force, violence and much argument in Britain's commercial and imperial interest.

The nation which the British left behind was supposed to be a federal democracy, but the federating ethnic nations were bound by few agreements and the peoples were so disparate, so culturally different, so varied in size, that force and violence seemed to be the only way of maintaining the nation. In the circumstances, the interests of the few and weak such as the Ogoni were bound to suffer and have suffered.

Petroleum was discovered in Ogoni in 1958 and since then an estimated US 100 billion dollars' worth of oil and gas has been carted away from Ogoni land. In return for this, the Ogoni people have received nothing.

Oil exploration has turned Ogoni into a waste land: lands, streams, and creeks are totally and continually polluted; the atmosphere has been poisoned, charged as it is with hydrocarbon vapours, methane, carbon monoxide, carbon dioxide and soot emitted by gas which has been flared 24 hours a day for 33 years in very close proximity to human habitation. Acid rain, oil spillages and oil blow-outs have devastated Ogoni territory. High-pressure oil pipelines criss-cross the surface of Ogoni farmlands and villages dangerously.

The result of such unchecked environment pollution and degradation include the complete destruction of the ecosystem. Mangrove forests have fallen to the toxicity of oil and are being replaced by noxious nypa and palms; the rainforest has fallen to the axe of the multinational oil companies; all wildlife is dead, marine life is gone, the farmlands have been rendered infertile by acid rain and the once beautiful Ogoni countryside is no longer a source of fresh air and green vegetables. All one sees and feels around is death. Environmental degradation had been a lethal weapon in the war against the indigenous people of Ogoni.

Incidental to and indeed compounding this ecological devastation is the political marginalisation and complete oppression of the Ogoni and especially the denial of their rights, including their land rights. At independence, Nigeria consisted of three regions. Since then, 30 states have been created largely for the ethnic majorities who rule the country. Most of the states so created are unviable and depend entirely on Ogoni resources for their survival. The demands of the Ogoni for autonomy and self-determination even within the Nigerian nation have been ignored. The Ogoni have been corralled into a multi-ethnic administrative state in which they remain a minority and therefore suffer several disabilities. Mining rents and royalties for Ogoni oil are not being paid to Ogoni people. In spite of the enormous wealth of their land the Ogoni people continue to live in primitive conditions in the absence of electricity, pipe-borne water, hospitals, housing and schools. The Ogoni are being consigned to slavery and extinction.

Faced by these terrible odds, the Ogoni people have continued courageously to demand social justice and equity. In October 1990 the Chiefs and leaders of Ogoni submitted a Bill of Rights to the Nigerian President and his council. They are yet to receive a reply to these minimum demands.

The extermination of the Ogoni people appears to be policy. The Ogoni have suffered at the hands of the military dictatorships which have ruled Nigeria over the past decades. The new constitution, which is supposed to usher in a democratic government in 1993, does not protect the rights of the Ogoni. Indeed, it institutionalises the expropriation of their land. A recently concluded national census omits all references to the ethnic origins of all citizens, which in a multi-ethnic state is a violation of community rights.

Nigeria has an external debt of over 30 billion dollars. None of that debt was incurred on any project in the Ogoni area or on any project remotely beneficial to the Ogoni. The International Monetary Fund and the World Bank, keen on the payment of the debt, are encouraging intensified exploitation of oil and gas, which constitute 94 per cent of Nigeria's gross domestic product. Such exploitation is against the wishes of the Ogoni people as it only worsens the degradation of the Ogoni environment and the decimation of the Ogoni people. Studies have indicated that more Ogoni people are dying now than are being born. The Ogoni are faced by a powerful combination of titanic forces from far and near, driven by greed and cold statistics. Only the international community, acting with compassion and a sense of responsibility to the human race, can avert the catastrophe which is about to overtake the Ogoni. The Ogoni people are now appealing to that community...

National ideas of national independence, the fact of Africans ruling Africans in nations conceived by and for European economic interests have intensified, not destroyed, the propensity of man to subject weak peoples by force, violence and legal quibbling to slavery and extinction. I respectfully invite you to visit Nigeria, so that you can see for yourself that indigenous peoples abound there and that they suffer incredibly at the hand of rulers and the economic interests of other nations.

I spent 10 to 12 days in Geneva that summer. I had holidayed there in the early 1980s with my sons, taking them on a tour of the United Nations buildings. I was then ignorant of its very important work. Now I saw for myself how backward Nigeria is in regard to the setting-up of non-governmental organisations and working through them for the protection of rights.

I also made valuable contacts with individuals and groups from other parts of the world. I came to know that the UN had busied itself for more than a decade with the problems of such peoples as the Ogoni (indigenous people) or national minorities in various countries. I ought to have been in Geneva much sooner.

One thing which struck me was the extent of misery among indigenous peoples throughout the world. Every case was very important to those who argued it, and it was possible to put one's concerns in a global perspective.

My address to the Working Group on Indigenous Populations was published in Nigerian newspapers. And this, I believe, is what may have convinced the Ogoni élite that there was some value in what I was doing. Many sceptics would have wondered what chance we had prosecuting our case against a powerful company like Shell and a fascist government like Babangida's which was bent on spending every single cent that came from oil; or, indeed, against the entire Nigerian élite, who didn't want to work but were living happily off the lottery which they had won in oil revenues, without worrying about the cost of earning such revenue.

After the Steering Committee of MOSOP was formally set up in early 1991, it was as if the signatories to the Bill of Rights had gone to sleep. Even when Babangida and his military colleagues showed their hands at their most insensitive and most bandit-like in creating additional states and local governments from which the Ogoni and others in the Rivers State were excluded, few seemed to worry.

And yet it was this act alone which so outraged me that I decided that, come life or death, the brutalisation of the peoples in the oil-bearing delta of the Niger would have to be questioned, exposed and brought to a stop. The way and manner in which the states and local governments were created were an affront to truth and civility, a slap in the face of modern history; it was robbery with violence. What Babangida was doing was transferring the resources of the delta, of the Ogoni and other ethnic minorities to the ethnic majorities – the Hausa-Fulani, the Igbo and the Yoruba – since most of the new states and local governments were created in the homes of these three. None of the local governments or states so created was viable: they all depended on oil revenues which were to be shared by the states and local governments according to the most outrageous of criteria such as expanse of land, equality, underdevelopment and all such stupidities. The brazen injustice of it hurts my sensibilities beyond description.

Ruminating over the development, and watching Nigeria literally go down the drain through the incompetence and banditry of the ruling military civilian politicians, I became stronger in my conviction that the only thing that could save Nigeria was the political restructuring of the country. Something had to be done to bring the urgency of the matter home.

My contact with UNPO in Geneva and other organisations and activists had introduced me to the nature of non-violent struggle for rights. And I already knew how successful the mobilisation movements in Nigeria had been once they were based on the ethnic group. Awolowo, Azikiwe and Ahmadu Bello had successfully mobilised their kinsmen, the Yoruba, the Igbo and the Hausa-Fulani respectively. I thought I could do the same for the Ogoni.

I quickly wrote and published a book, *Genocide in Nigeria: The Ogoni Tragedy*, which told the Ogoni story in urgent terms and called attention to its environmental and political problems.

Perhaps one reason the MOSOP Steering Committee had not worked effectively was the return of partisan politics. When we had signed the Bill of Rights in 1990, most Ogoni politicians, as I have said, had been banned from participation in politics. By 1991, the ban on a few of them had been lifted and this had seduced them away from the efforts of the MOSOP.

By 1992 Babangida's trickery and unpredictability, as he manoeuvred and fooled the Nigerian people, had lifted the ban on most politicians, although some of the older Ogoni politicians were still working with us in the MOSOP. We, however, recognised the need to broaden the base of our support beyond the signatories to the Bill of Rights and a few youths who had begun to attend meetings with us. So we organised a two-day tour of the Ogoni kingdoms, on 14 and 28 November 1992.

The results took me entirely by surprise. I hadn't mixed much with the youth of Ogoni over the years, since there was no organisation which took care of all Ogoni people. On that tour, I found that there was a large number of youth angry with a society that had cheated them and who were therefore eager to hear us, to learn. I have to explain that the term 'youth' is used here to describe people who are below the age of 40.

Generally, on our tour, we would introduce a motion calling upon Shell, Chevron and the Nigerian National Petroleum Corporation (NNPC), the three oil companies operating in Ogoni, to pay damages of US four billion dollars for destroying the environment, six billion dollars in unpaid rents and royalties; and all within 30 days or it would be assumed that they had decided to quit the land. The resolution was unanimously carried in the six kingdoms of Ogoni.

Two scenes will remain indelible in my memory because they gave me so much comfort and encouragement: the first was in 1992 at Bori, when we met at the Suanu Finimale Nwika Conference Centre, which was to become the scene of many a stirring meeting. There I found a very ready response and also highly intelligent questions from a very knowledgeable audience.

The second was at the secondary school in Kpor in the Gokana kingdom. The hall into which we were crammed proved too small and we had perforce to go into the open air. I spoke in one of the four Ogoni languages from the balcony of the upper floor of the secondary school building at Kpor in Gokana. And the response was immediate and overwhelming. From the reaction of the sea of faces down below, you would have thought that I had been lecturing them for years. Indeed, on reflection, I now realise what happened: I was not telling these people anything they had not known. I had only given

71

voice to the facts and fears they had harboured in their hearts for years but which they dared not express for fear of the expected reprisals which they knew the Nigerian state would not hesitate to visit on them.

Mr B M Wifa, one-time Attorney-General of Rivers State, an Ogoni man from Kono, has been a friend from our primary school days. Extremely bright, he excelled in mathematics and might have been an engineer had he wanted to. He chose the law, and since he could not find a bursary, and no-one in Ogoni was able to sponsor him, had to work and study in the United Kingdom for a long time before he finally became a lawyer. I relied a lot on his legal opinions, and I always gave him my non-fiction work to read to ensure that there was nothing libellous therein. I discussed my ideas on the Ogoni people with him regularly.

It was to him I turned in writing the 'Demand Notice' to the three oil companies. After he had vetted my draft, I sent off the letter on 3 December 1992, knowing full well that they would ignore it.

The four days prior to that I had spent with Ogoni youths preparing the ground for the massive protest march which we had planned for 4 January 1993.

The date, 4 January was significant, and it was carefully chosen. The disgraced dictator, Babangida, was expected to hand over power on 2 January 1993. If he did so, we would be serving notice to the new administration that the Ogoni people would no longer accept exploitation and a slave status in Nigeria. If Babangida failed to hand over, we would be confronting him directly and daring him to do his worst.

I travelled to London after submitting the 'Demand Notice' to the oil companies. My purpose was to attend the inauguration of the United Nations International Year for the World's Indigenous Populations in New York. On arrival in London, I found that it was not going to be possible to get to New York because of visa problems. I therefore spent the time convincing Greenpeace to send a team to watch the protest march for the environment planned for 4 January 1993 in Ogoni.

At first they wouldn't hear of it. But when I affirmed that I was expecting no less than 300,000 people to take part in the march, they finally agreed to send a cameraman. Shelley Braithwaite, an Australian member of the London-based Rainforest Action Group, also agreed to travel as my guest to Ogoni to participate in the march.

I returned to Nigeria shortly before Christmas. I stopped in Lagos to invite the press to Ogoni on 4 January before proceeding to Port Harcourt.

When I arrived there, I found considerable ferment in security circles over the planned demonstration. Dr Leton and Edward Kobani had earned the attention of the operatives of the notorious repressive SSS. On Christmas Day itself, early in the morning, Dr Leton rang me up.

'The SSS have invited me once again,' he moaned.

On Christmas Day?' I asked in astonishment.

'Yes.'

'What could they possibly want that couldn't wait until tomorrow or the day after?'

'God alone knows.'

'I'll come with you, if you don't mind,' I said.

I put on a shirt and headed for Dr Leton's. From there, we drove to the offices of the dreaded SSS. At the gate we inquired if the State Director was available. On being told that he was at his residence, we headed there. We had decided earlier not to deal with his subordinates as they were likely to mess around with us.

We met Mr Terebor, State Director of the SSS, on arrival. As is usual with me, I asked where he came from and found that he was of Ondo State (one of the six Yoruba states) origin. He had studied physics at the University of Ife and I could not, for the life of me, understand what he was doing in the notorious SSS when the country was crying out for teachers of physics in secondary schools. I believe that he said something about teaching not being rewarding.

We chatted generally and when we asked why we were being invited on Christmas Day to a security chat and were not allowed to enjoy the festival with our family, he apologised and offered us drinks. Then he telephoned his subordinates and two of them showed up. His immediate assistant was a Mr Egwi from Delta State and there was another operative from Enugu State. We spoke generally and I assured them that the Ogoni people and their leaders were not up to mischief but were celebrating the end of the year in their usual way. We offered to co-operate fully with them to ensure that there was no breach of the peace.

We parted on friendly terms. I headed home. Shortly after arrival there, the telephone rang and the voice of Rufus Ada George, Governor of Rivers State, came over the wire. He was inviting me, along with Dr Leton, to lunch in Government House.

Dr Leton and I arrived at Government House within minutes of each other. We found there almost the full complement of the Cabinet of Rivers State. I did not know many of them, beyond the Deputy Governor, Dr Odili, and my friend and fellow Ogoni, Dr Israel Kue. Also present was Dr Nwifa Ndegwe, another Ogoni man of whom I was decidedly not fond. In the early days when I was casting about for assistance in my struggle for the Niger River Delta environment, he gave me some support. But all he wanted me to do was to make noises abroad and not educate the victims of the degradation of the delta as to their rights to a healthy environment.

On that Christmas Day 1992, he was in his usual element, allowing me a place next to him at the Christmas dinner table, while his commissioners huddled silently together like rain-beaten hens at the far end of the table. It was a sumptuous meal too, complete with wines and champagne, all at public expense. Unused to such luxuries, I indulged myself fully. When I raised the matter of the invitation to the security office on Christmas Day of all days, he claimed to know nothing about it. Vile politician!

Two days later the Kagote Club honoured me with its first Ogoni National Merit Award at a ceremony which was held at Suanu Finimale Nwika Conference Centre in Bori. In my acceptance speech I said:

We have taken the first important step in clearing our minds, in achieving unity of leadership, in projecting our case before Nigeria. The next task is to mobilise every Ogoni man, woman and child on the nature and necessity of our cause, so that everyone knows and believes in that cause and holds it as a religion, refusing to be bullied or bribed therefrom. And finally, we must begin to build up action to transform our current advantages into political scores.

We have been faithful to this agenda which we set up for ourselves. We have established the Ogoni identity and placed Ogoni on the national agenda; we have to mobilise all Ogoni people. We must now move on to the next item on our list: to establish a government of Ogoni people by Ogoni people for Ogoni people in Ogoni within a federal Nigeria. This is very important because we cannot and should not tolerate a situation where our best men and women are exiled from our land; a situation where our genius is not being placed at the disposal of our land.

All successful Ogoni men and women are in Port Harcourt, Lagos or some such centre in Nigeria or overseas. To be in Ogoni means that you are not successful. Out in the diaspora, the Ogoni man is insignificant and is forced to bring up his children outside of Ogoni culture. It is not surprising that a new generation of highly-trained Ogoni men and women are growing up, marrying outside the tribe and raising another generation who are further alienated from the nation because they have not grown up within Ogoni culture and traditions. This is surely the path to the extinction of our nation.

General Babangida's kabukabu presidency, his kakistocracy, has been a complete failure and has spelled the death of the Ogoni and other delta peoples. His touted transition truck is completely rusty, without a road worthiness certificate or an insurance policy; its licence has expired. Yet, its driver insists on taking it out on an endless journey. The driver's licence needs renewal, but he insists on proceeding without it, depending on his ability to bribe the traffic policemen along the way. Loaded with touts, the truck stops at odd places to pick up stranded passengers. If an unwitting passenger complains later about the state of the truck, the touts shout him down, shut him up and threaten to offload him and leave him at the mercy of armed robbers. The touts, dependent on the driver for their 'chop' money, chant his praises even as he drives recklessly without a spare tyre or headlamps towards the precipice. I fear the truck, the driver and the touts, and I fear for the passengers. God grant that they do not involve innocent bystanders in a fatal accident. I advise everyone to stand far away from the possible paths of the deadly truck.

We must renew our faith in the Ogoni Bill of Rights and pursue the attainment of our rights in a non-violent manner. And we must get absolutely ready for the achievement of our desires, because the challenges which that achievement will pose are as tough as any that have gone before.

I have personally dedicated myself to the Ogoni nation. For me, the struggle is my first priority, taking precedence over all other interests. For I believe that the achievements of the Ogoni will serve as an example to other ethnic minorities and oppressed peoples throughout Africa.

I spent the following week in constant communication with Governor Ada George and the security agents. They didn't want the Ogoni protest march to go on. I didn't understand their doubts. The march was billed as a peaceful one. They argued that it would be violent. I didn't see how it would be. I asked that they monitor it closely and nip any tendency to violence in the bud. But they were as jittery as I was adamant.

In spite of Ada George (who, by virtue of his position, was Chairman of the Rivers State Security Council, which consisted of the army, navy, air force, police and SSS) we continued to plan the demonstration. The Greenpeace photographer, Tim Lambon, soon arrived and went to work filming the devastated Ogoni environment. He was not impeded in his work in any way.

As noted earlier, I was not quite aware of the level of expertise available among the young Ogoni. But as they clustered around me in my office and we planned the day, I began to learn one or two things about them. They were high on enthusiasm and dedicated to the cause we had outlined.

Then the usual doubts came from the usual quarters. Dr Leton began to plead that we call off the demonstration. Ogoni had been ringed round by the military. Babangida had decided not to hand over power and had given orders that there be no processions throughout the country. Anyone found in a march carrying placards would be shot. He claimed even to have had a dream in which he was shot while carrying a placard.

This manner of reasoning chilled me. I feared that it might infect the younger men and destroy the work of a whole year. I laid great store by the protest march: it was a psychological break point. If we could defy the authorities and successfully protest our denigration, the Ogoni would be on their way to a proper future.

As of Saturday, 2 January 1993, the debate was still going on. The planning committee, consisting of myself and some youths, was still at work, placards had been written and stored, loud-speaker equipment procured, and procedures laid down. But would we march? I called a meeting at Dr Leton's residence in Beeri, a few miles from the Bori headquarters of the Ogoni nation. And then God dropped from the skies.

He arrived in the person of a close family relation who informed us that he had, on his own, investigated the disposition of the troops in the area. The police and army were around all right, but they would not shoot unless they had given three warnings. In any case, they would shoot into the air before shooting into a crowd.

Right or wrong, it served to dispel all fears. From that moment onwards, no-one spoke of not marching for fear of the army or police. We concluded the meeting on a high note of optimism and dispersed to our various homes.

I checked with the co-ordinators we had appointed in each of the kingdoms to ensure that all was well. They confirmed that it was so. Four men, and, where possible, a woman had been assigned the task of forming committees in each village; and the village committees, in turn, had been given the responsibility of ensuring that everyone turned out for the protest march along with dance troupes, masquerades and all such.

One word about the festival aspect of the march. Joy should not have been a part of so serious and monumental a protest. But I was very worried about a number of things. True, we had told everyone that we were not going to be violent; that not a stone would be thrown. But how could we be sure that this would be carried out? Crowd control was another problem. If we could not keep the men, women and children who would turn out busy, then the devil would find them an occupation. Hence the decision to keep them entertained with spectacle and song. The other problem was what we would do if people were wounded or hurt. The hospital in Bori was no use at all. There was a fine Ogoni doctor there all right, John Nwidaada of Kpean, a gracious young man trained in Moscow, but he had no equipment. The hospital had been opened with fanfare in 1952. I was in our school's musical band at Bori, which was in attendance on the occasion. T N Paul Birabi had spoken on the day, outlining his hopes that the hospital would help provide medical care to all Ogoni people. His hopes were not borne out. Although the hospital started out well, it degenerated to the point where, by January 1993, it was no better than the dispensaries which each kingdom of the Ogoni had had in my childhood days.

There was not much we could do as far as medical

problems were concerned. My brother Owens' clinic had an ambulance and he, of course, volunteered it along with all his staff and his services. I had to hope for the best.

That Saturday we did not quite succeed in checking out all the arrangements. We scheduled another meeting for the next day, after the Sunday service of 3 January.

Chapter Five

W E had not initially thought of presaging the protest of 4 January with an inter-denominational service and a visit to the tomb of T N Paul Birabi. The inspiration for that came from Goodluck Diigbo, a journalist from Kaani who turned up at my office regularly and voluntarily to render invaluable advice on the public relations aspects of our endeavour. He was quite a godsend, being a good organiser and far more knowledgeable about the psyche of the Ogoni people at that time than I was. He lived among them; I did not. He also knew well the influence of radio as a mobiliser, working as he did in the state ration broadcasting station, Radio Rivers.

We made contact with the Venerable Archdeacon Ntor, a fine man who was, at the time, in charge of the Anglican Church in the Ogoni area. He was based at Yeghe, the birthplace of T N Paul Birabi and his tomb lay next to the church of St Peter's. The Venerable Ntor did not have any hesitation in organising the church service.

On the morning of Sunday, 3 January, I was up early and set off for Yeghe immediately after breakfast in the company of Alfred Ilenre, General Secretary of EMIROAF, who had come to witness the march, and my young friend Hauwa Madugu.

A word need be said here of Alfred, who was to help immensely in the Ogoni struggle. Of Ishan extraction, he had taken to journalism immediately upon leaving school in 1958 or thereabouts, and had worked on several Nigerian newspapers and subsequently in the Angolan Embassy in Lagos when that country was involved in its struggle for independence. A wise man, he had a thorough knowledge of Nigerian politics and had met and interviewed some of the best-known Nigerian politicians, including Obafemi Awolowo. I was also to benefit a lot from his deep insights into Nigerian life.

When we arrived at Yeghe that morning, only Venerable Ntor and a few choristers were around. My heart fell. I had expected that the people of Yeghe, if no-one else, would have milled around the church. One hour later, at about 10 o'clock, there were still only a few people around. We waited until eleven o'clock and still there were not enough worshippers. Venerable Ntor at that point decided that we would have to commence the service. My disappointment was real, but I found comfort in the fact that Dr Leton and Edward Kobani had arrived along with Bishop J B Poromon of the Methodist Church who was to preach the sermon.

I need not have worried. By the time the service had gone some way, the church was full to bursting and more worshippers had milled outside. Chiefs, women, men and children from all parts of Ogoni, including Eleme, which was far away, turned up to worship God and to pray for the success of our protest march.

What I remember best of that service was the lesson read by Ledum Mitee, who had lately begun to play a prominent role in the affairs of the MOSOP. The passage had been well-chosen by Venerable Ntor, from the Lamentations of Jeremiah, and I will beg the indulgence of the reader to reproduce it in full:

Remember, O Lord, what has befallen us; behold, and see our disgrace! Our inheritance has been turned over to strangers, our homes to aliens. We have become orphans, fatherless; our mothers are like widows. We must pay for the water we drink, the wood we get must be bought. With a yoke on our necks, we are hard driven; we are weary, we are given no rest. We have given the land to Egypt, and to Assyria, to get bread enough. Our fathers sinned, and are no more; and we bear their iniquities. Slaves rule over us; there is none to deliver us from their hand. We get our bread at the peril of our lives, because of the sword in the wilderness. Our skin is as hot as an oven with the burning heat of famine. Women are ravished in Zion, virgins in the towns of Judah. Princes are hung up by their hands; no respect is shown to the elders. Young men are compelled to grind at the mill; and boys stagger under loads of wood. The old men have quit the city gate, the young men their music. The joy of our hearts has ceased; our dancing has been turned to mourning. The crown has fallen from our head; woe to us, for we have sinned! For this our heart has become sick, for these things our eyes have grown dim, for Mount Zion which lies desolate; jackals prowl over it. But thou, O Lord, dost reign for ever, thy throne endures to all generations. Why dost though forget us for ever, why dost thou so long forsake us? Restore us to thyself, O Lord, that we may be restored! Renew our days as of old! Or has though utterly rejected us? Art though exceedingly angry with us?

I doubt that we could have found a passage of literature more apt for the Ogoni situation. And I was certainly not the only one in the Church that day who received the true tenor of the message. I could feel a slight tremor pass through the pews when Ledum finished reading.

Equally interesting was Bishop Poromon's (a Gokana man) sermon delivered in flawless Khana. By the end of the service, I found myself greatly encouraged and imbued with a new energy and faith.

When we finally trooped to Birabi's grave, the crowd had become virtually unmanageable, but I was introduced to the tremendous discipline of the Ogoni people which was to be shown the next day. At the first greeting hailing everyone, silence reigned and all movement stopped.

There were several speeches. In mine, I stressed the fact that we were out on a non-violent struggle for our rights, that I wouldn't want any blood spilled in that struggle, and that we would no longer allow what happened to the Amerindians, the Australian Aborigines and the New Zealand Maoris to happen to us. I assured the Ogoni people of eventual victory.

The speech was meant to challenge the Nigerian system and to encourage the Ogoni people to resist their denigration. And I was pleased when I observed that the Lagos press had sent its representatives to follow the event.

My only and greatest sadness was the conspicuous absence of Bennet Birabi from both the church and his late father's tomb. It was a betrayal which I knew would haunt the fellow for ever. And I knew that the Ogoni people would never forget it.

The meeting scheduled to be held at Beeri after the church service was well attended, far more so than that of the previous day. It was held in the residence of Chief Ema Apenu, an engineer, and a cousin of Dr Leton. There being so much enthusiasm around, all we had to do was put final touches to the arrangements we had on the ground.

Each Ogoni kingdom had six co-ordinators and each village four, to plan and streamline activities and movement. As indicated earlier, we decided to put some entertainment into our activities to eliminate the possibility of violence. We had detailed the making of posters, banners and placards to various youths.

The main protest was to take place at Bori, the headquarters of the Ogoni nation. Ordinarily, the ride to Port Harcourt should take no more than 30 minutes. There isn't a single hill on the way. But the road was in such terrible disrepair that going on it was like an obstacle course. The journey time tripled. It hurt sorely to think how much money Ogoni was belching forth and how such a short stretch of road could not be made motorable. In Abuja, the new Nigerian capital, oil money was being used to blast stones, break hills and build roads which were hardly in use.

Arriving in Port Harcourt the evening before, I had a quick

dinner and repaired to my office to prepare the address I was to make at Bori the following morning. We had arranged that in addition to Dr Leton's speech as President, other speeches would be made by me, Ledum Mitee representing the youth of Ogoni and by a woman who was yet to be identified. I had asked Joy Nunieh, the lovely, humorous, young lawyer, to prepare a draft address on behalf of Ogoni women.

All that night I spent either writing my speech or editing the other speeches. My staff were on leave, besides its being a Sunday, and I had to work alone on the computer in the office. Alfred Ilenre was around to keep me company and to encourage me whenever I showed signs of wilting.

The speeches were ready by four that morning and I repaired to bed quite exhausted. By six o'clock I was up again. I had no appetite for breakfast and tended to be at the very short end of a fuse, being brusque with all those who were unfortunate enough to be around me. Most of them probably understood how I felt and made allowance for it.

We set off for Bori shortly after seven o'clock. My intent was to stop at the headquarters of all the six Ogoni kingdoms but it was necessary to have all the Ogoni leaders together. I therefore decided to drive directly to Beeri.

The road was remarkably quiet. It was Monday morning, the first working day of the year after the Christmas and New Year festivities. Ordinarily, a lot of people should have been returning to Port Harcourt, and not only from the Ogoni area, but also from Opobo, Andoni and Ibibioland. But we did not pass a single vehicle until we got to Bori.

There were a few banners along the road, proclaiming the day as 'Ogoni Day in the International Year of the World's Indigenous People'. Shortly before Bori, at Yeghe, we began to see signs of the readiness of the people to march. A number of youths, men and women were already forming groups, holding twigs, the symbol of the environment which we had chosen. My brother Owens was already on the road, in his ambulance, monitoring what was going on.

I drove into Beeri and handed over Dr Leton's speech to him. He had been waiting for me and told me his cousin, Engineer Apenu, had already left for Tabangh, the headquarters of Nyo-Khana kingdom, on foot!

Thereafter, I drove to Mogho, at the centre of Gokana kingdom, where I was to meet the first glorious sight of that day. It was a little past nine o'clock. Tim Lambon, the Greenpeace photographer, and Shelley Braithwaite of the Rainforest Action Group, who was my guest in Port Harcourt, had begun photographing in the area, as was their wont, well before seven o'clock.

As I drove up, a huge crowd, the largest I had seen in my life up to that moment, emerged from the different roads which led to the primary school at Mogho, whose football field was to be the venue for the rally. They had apparently been at work since seven o'clock and had gone to K Dere, the site of the Bomu oilfield, to symbolically take over the oilfield with its flaming gas flare. All the Shell workers had abandoned the area the previous day.

They bore down, these poor, denigrated Ogoni people, green twigs, banners or placards in their hands, songs on their lips, and anger in their legs and faces, moving in an endless stream to the Mogho playground. But there was also pride in their faces, and I felt incredibly proud with them. It was with a lot of effort that I stopped the tears which welled up in me from streaming down my face. The empowerment which had enabled them to stand up to their oppressors at long last was the issue of the day.

The youths would not allow me to walk from my car to the venue of the rally. They insisted on carrying me shoulder-high to the rostrum, where I was expected to address the teeming and excited crowd.

On arrival at the rostrum, another problem reared its head: crowd control. There was a real possibility that the rostrum might collapse, or that the crowd pressing forward to get a glimpse or to be close to the centre of action might crush me and others.

In the event; none of that happened, I was able to silence the crowd after hailing them with the traditional 'M kana mon Gokana!' ('I salute all Gokana!'). Edward Kobani spoke, congratulating them on having taken over the oilfields symbolically. He himself had been at the head of the action, which was a great thing for a man of his age. And he asked, 'Did not the thieves run away the moment, we, the owners of the property, showed up to reclaim it?' 'They did!' replied the crowd enthusiastically, and the arena was drowned in cheers and handclaps. I felt ever so proud of my friend, the great Ogoni patriot he has always been.

I then spoke briefly, in the Gokana tongue, outlining the reason we were marching, and assuring them that no matter how long the battle lasted, we should all be ready to fight because there was no alternative to struggle. I congratulated them on the achievement of the day, assuring them that victory would assuredly be ours in the long term.

I had to save myself for the speeches I would be making at the other centres. The sun had already risen high in the sky and the air was thick with humidity. Sweat glistened on all faces and the dust rose into the air, adding to our discomfort.

I was carried from the rostrum on the shoulders of Ogoni youths back to my waiting car in a very slow procession. I got to the car eventually, but then the youths would not let the car move, insisting on sitting on the bonnet, blocking the view of my chauffeur as he tried to move off.

As we inched forward, a helicopter flew over the rally ground and a solitary policeman walked towards us in a friendly sort of way. I was quite worried for him, as I was for the pick-up van with a number of police personnel that drove past us in the opposite direction towards the local police station. I know that the place was crawling with over a thousand policemen; I was later to learn that they had not been paid a salary or out-of-station allowances. In any case, they kept out of sight that whole day; those who showed up fraternised openly with the marchers.

We were able, eventually, to leave the Mogho area streaming with sweat. We headed towards Tai kingdom. There were now several cars on the road, headed towards the different rally venues. When we got to Kira where the Tai kingdom rally was to be held, the venue was also full of people who were drumming, singing and dancing.

Dr Leton had now joined up, and he addressed the crowd briefly, after Mr Noble Obani-Nwibari, the foremost Tai activist, had introduced him. I spoke thereafter, in my Khana mother-tongue, drawing enthusiastic cheers. Noble took the rostrum after me, and when he was done we left for Bori, where the biggest rally was scheduled to take place.

The ride into Bori was a pleasurable one, that stretch of road being quite smooth and short. The road was chock-a-block with people, old and young, moving on foot towards Bori. As we got close to the venue of the rally, the Birabi Memorial Grammar School playground, the crowd thickened. It was, of course, a much bigger crowd than that at Gokana, and you would have thought that all of Ogoni was present on the field that day. And yet there were still people waiting at two other centres – at Baen in Ken-Khana kingdom and Tabangh in Nyo-Khana kingdom.

It was well-nigh impossible to find a way through the crowd, which raised an enormous amount of dust, and since my car was not air-conditioned the discomfort was high. We rolled up the car windows and steamed in the car as we inched forward. We finally got to the VIP area and I alighted to the delirious cries of the marchers. The cream of Ogoni society, less the government-paid traditional rulers and party politicians, was present and the atmosphere was euphoric.

Drummers thumped away at the far end of the arena and dance troupes performed skilfully. I shook hand with the chiefs and other leaders present. The crowd milled towards the VIP stand and we were at pains to keep the canopies standing. Controlling the crowd was becoming a problem. I guessed that the sooner we got started, the sooner we would be done and so prevent any accidents or incidents. I motioned to the appointed Master of Ceremonies to get started.

Chiefs Gbarazian of Bori, Gbaranee of Yeghe and Apere of Kaani jointly poured libation in the traditional Ogoni manner, calling on the gods of the land to bless our endeavour.

Thereafter, Dr Leton was introduced and he read his speech, which reminded the government that the Ogoni people were not asking for the moon but for their rights, including the right to modern amenities of life and to survival.

Miss Joy Nunieh followed him, outlining the considerable difficulties the women faced in a situation of environmental disaster and economic strangulation.

Speaking after her, Mr Ledum Mitee, representing the youth of Ogoni, assured the crowd that the youth were out to defend their patrimony and that no prison could stop them from pressing home their claim.

I noticed that the press were fully represented. I had seen the team from *Newswatch* magazine, consisting of a reporter and a photographer, at Yeghe, the previous day. Here, there were others from various newspapers and radio. We had commissioned a team of videotape photographers, and they were also at work. Someone whom I did not know at the time but whom I was to know better thereafter, Mr Meshack Karanwi of Baen, a lecturer in Communication Arts at the University of Port Harcourt, had turned up with the most eloquent statement at the rally – a burnt Nigerian flag – which he held on a pole over the heads of all the speakers.

When it was my turn to speak, I mounted the rostrum and sized up the crowd. From a vantage point above everyone, I saw a new profile of the Ogoni people, a profile I had not identified. I saw eagerness, determination and joy on the young faces that looked up to the men on the rostrum. And I knew that a new seed had germinated and everything would have to be done to water, nurture, grow and harvest it. Ogoni would surely not be the same again. And I also felt that I must not let them down ever, or they would be right to lynch me!

The dust in the arena was incredible, as dancers, masqueraders and revellers continued their celebration through other speeches. I wanted and demanded silence and got it. When the arena was absolutely still, I decided not to speak in English, but in Khana, starting with a solidarity song 'Aaken, aaken, pya Ogoni aaken!' ('Arise, arise, Ogoni people arise!'). I had written the song in the days of the civil war in 1968/9. In the new Ogoni movement, it was sung with the right fist clenched and punching the air at the shoulder level. It called the Ogoni people to work, to study, to struggle, vowing that they would no longer tolerate oppression. Later, an Ogoni activist added the notion of joy to it.

My prepared speech included these words:

The year 1993 has been formally declared the International Year of the World's Indigenous People as directed by the General Assembly of the United Nations. The opening ceremonies took place in New York on 10 December 1992, International Human Rights Day. The event was co-sponsored by the Centre for Human Rights, the International Labour Office, United Nations Development Programme, United Nations Environment Programme, United Nations Children's Fund and UNESCO.

The declaration of the Year signifies the interest which the fate of indigenous people is receiving in the international community. Although the case of indigenous people in America, Australia and New Zealand is well known, indigenous people in Africa have received scant attention. EMIROAF hopes to fill this vacuum and it is to this end that we have given full support to the efforts of the Ogoni people to draw attention to their plight. We intend to organise further activities during this year.

Contrary to the belief that there are no indigenous people in Black Africa, our research has shown that the fate of such groups as the Zangon Kataf and Ogoni in Nigeria are, in essence, no different from those of the Aborigines of

Australia, the Maori of New Zealand and the Indians North of South America. Their common history is of usurpation of their land and resources, the destruction of their culture and the eventual decimation of the people. Indigenous people often do not realise what is happening to them until it is too late. More often than not, they are the victims of the actions of greedy outsiders. EMIROAF will continue to mobilise and represent the interest of all indigenous people on the African continent. It is in this regard that we have undertaken to publicise the fate of the Ogoni people in Nigeria.

The Ogoni are embattled and imperilled. Since oil was discovered in the area in 1958, they have been the victims of a deadly ecological war in which no blood is spilled, no bones are broken and no-one is maimed. But people die all the time. Men, women and children are at risk; plants, wild-life and fish are destroyed, the air is poisoned, and finally the land dies. Today Ogoni has been reduced to a waste land.

Unfortunately, the international community has not yet awakened fully to the grim nature of this sophisticated, if unconventional, battle. For a multinational oil company, Shell, to take over US 30 billion dollars from the small, defenceless Ogoni people and put nothing back but degradation and death is a betrayal of all humanity.

For the Nigerian government to usurp the resources of the Ogoni and legalise such theft by military decree is armed robbery.

To deny the Ogoni the right to self-determination and impose on them the status of slaves in this country is morally indefensible.

The stunning silence and insensitivity, the primitive harassment and intimidation which the looters of Lagos and the bandits of Abuja have visited on the Ogoni people since they began to demand their rights peacefully indicate that the Nigerian Government lacks the ability or will to solve the problem and that only the international community can help the Ogoni people.

I therefore call upon that community once again to come to the aid of the Ogoni before they are driven to extinction by the combined activity of the multinational oil companies and the oppressive, greedy rulers of Nigeria.

Oil has been mined in Ogoni since 1958. It is a wasting asset. When the oil finally runs out in ten years or so, what will the Ogoni people do? Who will come to their aid? Something must be done NOW to save Ogoni.

I congratulate the Ogoni people on their taking upon themselves the historic responsibility for saving themselves, their land and their environment, late in the day as this may have been.

I call upon you, my brothers and sisters, to fight relentlessly for your rights. As our cause is just, and God being our helper, we shall emerge victorious over the forces of greed, wickedness and obduracy.

The tenor of my extempore speech was that we would have to face both the rulers of Nigeria and Shell which had denigrated us and laid great burdens on individual Ogoni people. I declared Shell *persona non grata* and challenged them to kill off all Ogoni men, women and children before taking any more oil from Ogoni. I ended with a call upon all other oil-producing areas in the country to follow the Ogoni example. 'Rise up now and fight for your rights!'

By the time I was done, I was virtually wilting, it had been a particularly hot and humid day, and there wasn't anything – cold water or soft drink – in sight, I returned to my seat, heard one or two other speeches, and, almost fainting, made for my car.

Again, moving out of the arena proved quite a feat as children milled all over my car, chanting in Khana, and it was a very tired man indeed who finally found the gate of the school compound and, turning right, headed back to Port Harcourt.

I returned to Port Harcourt, the press corps following closely on my heels. Arriving home, I ordered and drank a full and welcome bottle of beer, granted a few interviews to the pressmen and then retired to bed. It was about four o'clock, but I had had enough for one day.

Memories of the march were to linger in my mind for a long time. Almost two thirds of the Ogoni population had marched peacefully. Those who could not go to the central venues had marched in their village squares. It was a great dance of the anger of the people. Not a stone was thrown, and no-one was hurt. Some of the youths, out of misguided enthusiasm, did stop travellers going to Port Harcourt to work. But apart from that, there were no incidents whatsoever.

Now, when I look back upon the day, I feel very proud of being an Ogoni man. Ours was a great feat, even if I say so.

That day, 4 January, was a truly liberation day: a day on which young and old, able and disabled, rich and poor, all of Ogoni came out to reassert themselves and to give notice that the nation had come of age – that it would not accept its destruction passively. We had surmounted the psychological barrier of fear. Ogoni would never be the same again.

And I thought how wonderful it would be for Nigeria, for Africa, if the various ethnic nations that make it up could assert themselves in similar ways. We would be heading for a more democratic system far from the dictatorships which have ruined the continent; and we might succeed in reordering our societies, so that there would not be so much exploitation at all levels in all parts of the continent.

Somewhere, deep down in my heart, I hoped that I had started a movement which might transform Africa. Would the Ogoni revolution be a model for other small, deprived, dispossessed and disappearing peoples? If only we could make it! A large number of communities ready to take their fate into their hands and practise self-reliance, demanding their rights non-violently, would conduce to democracy and more politically developed peoples. The leaders of such peoples would no longer be able to take them for granted and cheat them and oppress them without remorse.

Chapter Six

IF I thought that there would be no answer to the march by those we had challenged, I was greatly mistaken. And, as usual, the first persons to be used were the Ogoni people themselves. A few of them were very close to Governor Ada George and were benefiting from his being in power. And it was to them he turned for assistance to wreak his revenge on the Ogoni people.

Their agreeing to do his dirty job for him was no surprise. The other man who joined them was unexpected. The late Albert Badey, the son of a Methodist priest, a fine man whom I knew well as a child, had studied at the Methodist College, Uzuakoli, where he was a great success, eventually securing a competitive scholarship to the University College, Ibadan. He thereafter joined the administrative service of the former Eastern Region and was well set to rise to the top of it. The civil war, in which he was on the Biafran side, sent him back to the Rivers State Civil Service in January 1970. He did Ogoni proud in the service.

The problem with Albert Badey was that he was a dyed-in-the-wool gerontocrat. The older a man is, the wiser. And he did not believe in the masses. A few people could always take decisions for the latter and all would be well. This attitude derived, I think, from his training as a civil servant. For Albert was a superb bureaucrat, dedicated to his career, and anxious not to rock the boat; any boat.

He rose steadily to the position of Permanent Secretary, the top of the Civil Service, and following the topsy-turvy methods of the military government, became Chairman of the Public Commission, then a commissioner and, by the time we started the Ogoni movement in 1990, was Secretary to the Rivers State government, the highest position anyone could achieve in the Civil Service. In short, Albert had achieved everything a man could achieve at the local level. He hungered for more, I think, and was young and talented enough to expect more. Had he been from anywhere else but Ogoni, he would have gone much further. Being an Ogoni, he was merely left to fester at the local level.

By 1993 when we intensified the Ogoni struggle, he was out of government. He was a great example of how the individual success of an Ogoni man could not make a difference to the generality of the Ogoni people.

As we were being flown to Lagos, the Ogoni friends of Governor Ada George were assembled at Bono Beach on Saturday, 9 January, to react to the protest march. I had been invited to the meeting, along with Dr Leton and Edward Kobani. Our absence did not stop them from holding the meeting. Albert, who, until then, had stayed resolutely away from the movement, was among them, along with a gaggle of government chiefs who had signed the Ogoni Bill of Rights but stayed away from the march of 4 January. The communiqué, signed by the chiefs, which they issued at end of their meeting in Kono appeared to take the side of the government against the Ogoni people. It included these words:

That [the Ogoni people,] in seeking for their right and appropriate treatment by the government, reaffirm their faith in the Federal Republic of Nigeria and reconfirm their commitment to peaceful pursuit of their grievances as the demonstration of Monday, 4 January 1993 fully proved. That the Ogoni people are aware of the recent encouraging actions of the Federal government in establishing Oil

Mineral Producing Areas Development Commission and they express their happiness about this development. In view of this, it is their expectation that our President and Commander-in-Chief of the Armed Forces of the Federal Republic will grant the Ogoni people audience for a reasoned presentation of their demand. Consequently, no further demonstration will be held in expectations of the positive reaction of government to their cry.

Those of us who travelled to Lagos were shocked to find this communiqué advertised in the government newspaper, *Nigerian Tide*. We knew who was behind it all.

On 17 January we quickly called another meeting of all the signatories of the Ogoni Bill of Rights at the Beeri residence of Engineer Apenu. And everyone recommitted themselves to the movement and reaffirmed that MOSOP was the only organisation responsible for the well-being of the Ogoni people and therefore authorised to speak and act on their behalf.

The day after this declaration was signed, I left for The Hague to attend a meeting of UNPO. The Ogoni people were admitted to the organisation by the Third General Assembly and I was elected Vice-Chairman of the Assembly. UNPO gave us the opportunity to appear on the world scene and CNN, the American world-wide television network, showed a slice of the Ogoni march, which Nigerians had not been able to see on their own television screens. And, for the first time, Ogoni appeared in *Time* magazine.

At the meeting, I attended a workshop on non-violent struggle. I recall the shock of one of our lecturers, a Palestinian, after hearing the Ogoni story from me. He had not ever thought that any group of people could be worse treated than his own people. I also introduced him to another type of violence: environmental degradation; and I did ask whether there was anything in the books as to how it could be confronted in a non-violent manner. No-one, it appeared, had ever thought of it.

I also met an official of Shell at the assembly and in a private discussion with him suggested that Shell would do well to ally itself with the owners of the land on which it operates rather than seek co-operation of bandit governments. I doubted that the message sank in. Indeed, it did not.

Shortly after that meeting, Shell International's Public Affairs Department summoned to London and to The Hague two of its top Nigerian managers, Nnaemeka Achebe, General Manager, Business, and a Mr Okonkwo of the Health and Safety Department, where they devised plans for dealing with the menace of Ken Saro-Wiwa and the Ogoni people.

They had not forgotten that I had called their environmental record in Ogoni into question in the documentary *The Heat of the Moment*, which was screened in London in October 1992. The minutes of their meeting which came into my hands subsequently indicated that 'key players', such as myself, were to be closely watched, our movements and actions followed closely throughout the world to ensure that we did not 'embarrass' Shell. I knew that Shell would revert to its usual acceptance of the government apparatus being used against us while stating that it knew nothing whatever about what was happening.

I began to think my life was seriously at risk. I was, however, ready for such a development, and wrote my will and informed my family that they should prepare for the worst. Nor did I ever fail, in my public speeches to the Ogoni people, to warn them to expect unsavoury developments from the Nigerian government. Later events were to prove me dead right.

On my return to Nigeria from The Hague via London, Dr Leton, Edward Kobani and I were summoned to Abuja on 14 February to meet the Director-General of the State Security Service, Mr Peter Ndiokwu. Glittering in lovely robes in the newly constructed ornate office of the service in Abuja, he read us the riot act. He particularly warned me in regard of my writings and press interviews. I assured him that I was merely drawing government attention to certain of its responsibilities and, as to his warning of the possibility of detention, I was quite ready to face the consequences of my actions.

When I returned to Ogoni the next week, it was to launch the One Naira Ogoni Survival Fund (ONOSUF), by which we sought to commit Ogoni men, women and children to the struggle. At the launch at Bori, on 27 February 1993, I gave the following Call to Commitment:

Almost three years ago, the chiefs and people of this blessed land took the first steps of an historic journey when, here in Bori, we formally established the Movement for the Survival of the Ogoni People (MOSOP) with the aim of extricating all Ogoni people from the shackles of indigenous colonialism and environmental strangulation, and of challenging the obnoxious, disgraceful and oppressive system imposed by successive military regimes on the peoples of Nigeria.

Since that day three years ago, the Ogoni people have established their identity as a distinct and unique people, reclaimed their right to freedom and independence, successfully placed their case before the international community, and put past and present rules of Nigeria before the bar of world opinion, where judges do not take bribes and rules cannot enact obnoxious decrees to imprison justice.

Today, the Ogoni people are involved in two grim wars. The first is the 35-year-old ecological war waged by the multinational oil companies, Shell and Chevron. In the most sophisticated and unconventional war, no bones are broken, no blood is spilled and no-one is maimed. Yet, men, women and children die; flora and fauna perish, the air and waters are poisoned, and finally, the land dies.

The second war is a political war of tyranny, oppression and greed designed to dispossess the Ogoni people of their rights and their wealth and subject them to abject poverty, slavery, dehumanisation and extinction.

Taken together, both wars, waged against the defenceless and small people, amount to genocide and are a grave crime against humanity.

Pitted against two deadly, greedy, insensitive and powerful enemies, the Ogoni people have refused to yield and are fighting doggedly and heroically for survival. And the war must be won, for the alternative to victory is extinction.

Our goal has been set out in the Ogoni Bill of Rights, where we underlined our determination to achieve political autonomy, the right to use our economic resources for our development, the right to protect the Ogoni environment and ecology from further degradation and the right to adequate and direct representation *as of right* in all Nigerian national institutions.

For the avoidance of doubt, let me reiterate that this last item underlines our desire to remain within the Nigerian nation-state. This decision has been taken, not because we think that secession is wrong, not for fear that the Nigerian constitution regards secession as treason (we are quite prepared to defy that constitution when necessary and to face the consequences of such defiance), but because we firmly believe in the brotherhood of black people world-wide and in sharing the blessings of God on an equitable basis with all.

MOSOP has an underlying social philosophy: ERECTISM, an acronym for Ethnic Autonomy, Resource and Environmental Control. We believe that under this umbrella, there will not only be self-reliance, democracy, social justice, healthy competition and progress, but that the Nigerian confederation which it proposed can be widened to embrace other African people in unity, peace and prosperity based on hard work.

The alternative to ERECTISM is dictatorship, retrogression and disintegration of the Nigerian nation-state. Those who therefore cling dishonestly to the frightening failures which characterise today's Nigeria because it works for them, are riding the horse of disaster. In the event of the disintegration of Nigeria, they will suffer the most.

In pursuance of the laudable goals of ERECTISM, we in the Ogoni are reconstructing our society even as we fight the grim war of genocide. We aim to: rehabilitate and reconstruct our proud heritage – the Ogoni nation – which has suffered enormous setbacks in the course of the life of this country; ensure our cultural survival by regenerating our traditional means of securing happiness, social interaction and well-being; re-emphasise the practice of self-reliance for which our forebears were noted; and ensure the study of our languages, Eleme, Gokana and Khana.

One of the first steps to this end is the establishment of the One Naira Ogoni Survival Fund. Why one naira we might ask?

The Ogoni people are an extremely rich but dispossessed people. In establishing this fund, we want to emphasise not money but the symbols of togetherness, of comradeship, of unity of endeavour, of the total commitment of young and old. Money cannot win the war of genocide against the Ogoni people. God Himself will win the war for us. But all Ogoni men, women and children, including newborn babies, will contribute to the Fund as a statement of their will to survive as individuals and as one indivisible nation.

The cost of reconstruction and recovery of the Ogoni nation is estimated to exceed US 15 billion dollars. We will have to find that money. In accordance with the political will of our people and in total condemnation of the deliberate and wicked exploitation of the Ogoni by the Nigerian nation-state and her agents, the Fund will not accept donations from any government in Nigeria. However, our friends at home and abroad, are welcome to contribute towards the reconstruction and rehabilitation process in Ogoni.

Over the last three years, the Nigerian government has shown a remarkable lack of will to do anything to mitigate the agony of the Ogoni. A government which routinely doles out millions of naira to minor social organisations and girlfriends has found it easy to ignore the death of thousands of Ogoni children, whose inheritance it is dissipating recklessly. Certainly, the problems which the rulers of Nigeria have inflicted on the Ogoni people are so monumental and daunting that the Nigerian nation-state cannot even contemplate them. Therefore, only the international community, working through the United Nations, can stop this genocide, this savagery so unworthy of the twenty-first century.

I appeal to you all to contribute to the Fund not only the sum of one naira but, much more importantly, your total commitment and dedication. For we are witnessing the birth of a new phenomenon: the decision by a small group of people that they will not tolerate their dehumanisation even by people of the same colour of skin. And that all the guns of the world, the casuistry of dictatorship and the threat of death and imprisonment cannot deter a people determined to secure their God-given rights and protect their inheritance.

The following month, on 13 March, we held a night vigil throughout the Ogoni nation. The Christian Church has a powerful hold in Ogoni, and the arrival of the Pentecostal Churches at a time of serious economic difficulties had led to even more people seeking solace in religion.

I drove into Bori at six o'clock that evening, and already Ogoni youths had massed up at the Birabi Memorial Grammar School playground. As the sun dipped in the west, a candle-lit procession took off. In an orderly single file, the youths marched through the length of Bori chanting: 'Go down, go down, go down to Abuja/And tell government, government, let Ogoni go!' They ended up at the Suanu Finimale Nwika

Conference Hall at the other end of town, where the Bori vigil took place. For reasons of crowd control, we had decided to keep the Bori crowd small and had instructed that the vigil take place in all Ogoni villages and towns simultaneously.

It was a very successful night, and as many of the Ogoni élite as possible were present at Bori. It was perhaps the last thing on which the group were agreed, it being harmless. The one thing I remember of it is that my 89-year-old father was with us until four o'clock the next morning. Most of the élite stole away at midnight. The rest of us continued until daybreak.

On the ides of March, the sad news came of the sudden death of my youngest son, Tedum. I had to go to England to complete the funeral obsequies of my lovely, 14-year-old boy, whose soul, please God, may find eternal, peaceful rest.

I had a commitment to lecture Itsekiri students in Warri on 3 April, and in spite of the pain I had in my heart, I returned from London and drove to Warri to keep the appointment. I arrived to find 20 policemen waiting to show me out of the town like some vermin. As I have said, they actually deported me from Delta State, seeing me across the Niger at the Patani Bridge and back into Rivers State. My first arrest.

From that moment onwards, I was in real trouble with Babangida's bloodhounds. When the federal government sent a team to Port Harcourt ostensibly to dialogue with people from the oil-producing areas, I was not allowed to speak on behalf of the Ogoni people. I had a chance to say all that was in my mind later that night when Governor Ada George invited me to a dinner at which the then Minister of Petroleum, Mr Asiodu, and other representatives of the NNPC and the government would be present.

I was happy to be able to confront Mr Asiodu, whose statement about the marginalisation of the ethnic minorities in the oil-bearing delta is the most insensitive, callous and provocative statement on record: 'Given the small size and population of the oil-producing areas, it is not cynical to

101

observe that even if the resentment of oil-producing states continue, they cannot threaten the stability of the country or affect its continued economic development'. He argued that he had not meant what he said. I disputed him, stressing that by no analysis whatsoever could any positive construction be put on the words by which he posited that the people of the Niger Delta could be exploited and denigrated.

Not allowing me to speak to the public appeared to be the play of government. I was, in short, being denied my right to freedom of expression. But the ideas were abroad, and I did not see how they could be stanched. The government had other ideas.

On 18 April, I was returning from a trip to Lagos when the security agents came tapping my shoulder at the Port Harcourt Airport. They took me to their shabby headquarters, searched my offices and home, seized a mass of documents and tapes and released me 18 hours later. My second arrest.

Five days later, they returned to my office and seized me at about noon. My third arrest. Mr Terebor, the Director, no, misdirector, of the SSS in Rivers State queried and questioned me about an Ogoni flag, an Ogoni National Anthem, the UNPO, and so on and so forth. He was obviously trying to establish a case for treason, secession being treasonable under Nigerian law.

Of course, there was nothing treasonable in the Ogoni demands. The Ogoni Bill of Rights had expressly stated as follows: 'now, therefore, while reaffirming our wish to remain a part of the Federal Republic of Nigeria, we make demand upon the republic as follows...' Only an idiot, or a man fishing for trouble, could ever construe those words as secessionist. Mr Terebor was no idiot and his subordinates were quite intelligent, as my conversation with them showed. So, what dirty job were they up to?

I was kept in their office for hours and questioned endlessly. Having not had a meal all day, I collapsed shortly after seven o'clock in the evening. When I began to feel bad, I asked for a doctor but they could not produce one. Only after I had collapsed did they let me go, but with instructions that I not leave Port Harcourt. In short, I was under town arrest.

That incensed the Ogoni people. Ogoni youths in Port Harcourt decided to stage a peaceful protest against the authorities and made arrangements to present a petition to the Rivers State House of Assembly.

At about six o'clock in the morning of the 29 April, one of my relatives came to my residence to inform me that the Police Mobile Force had surrounded my office and that it was advisable that I keep out of the area that day. I thanked him for his advice and remained in bed that morning till late.

In spite of the blandishments of the security agencies, who also mounted a guard at the entrance of the House of Assembly, the march went on as planned. Large numbers of them slipped into the premises of the secretariat pretending to be government workers.

By the time the assembly went into session, a rousing song rent the quiet air and protesters marched into the entrance of the assembly. Employees in the secretariat were taken by surprise and rushed to see what was happening.

Ogoni youths were making their protest heard as the assembly speaker came forward to receive the Ogoni petition demanding that the leaders be no longer harassed. Thereafter, they marched in a peaceful procession, holding aloft their Bibles, along the streets of Port Harcourt to the motor part on the Port Harcourt-Aba Expressway.

The march showed the remarkable organising ability of Ogoni youths and their determination to use all the instruments of non-violent struggle in the demand for Ogoni rights.

The message must have fallen on deaf ears. In any case, the battle was already joined, and we were probably no longer in control of whatever happened or was to happen. We were, from that day, largely reacting to what our opponents did

The very next day, on 30 April, disaster struck. Shell had been dualising the Trans-Niger pipeline, which carries oil from most parts of delta through Ogoni territory to the export terminal at Bonny. They had not carried out an environmental impact assessment. They had not negotiated with the landlords whose land they were using and desecrating. They simply got soldiers of the Nigerian army to guard them, who then bribed their way through any complaining villagers.

The soldiers had gone through a number of Ogoni villages, but when they got to Biara, where a major oil spill had polluted streams and the land two years earlier, incensed villagers, mostly women, turned out to question them. The women held twigs as they had been advised to do to indicate that they were protesting peacefully. The soldiers emptied their live ammunition on them. Eleven people were wounded, among them Mrs Karalole Korgbara, a mother of five children who was shot in the left arm – it was subsequently amputated.

If the powers that be thought that this would scare the Ogoni people, they were mistaken. The next day, thousands of unarmed Ogoni people poured into the site, daring the soldiers to shoot. This was too much for the stomachs of the American engineers who were working for the American pipeline contractor firm, Wilbros, which subsequently withdrew from the site. But not before the soldiers had murdered another man, Agbarator Otu, who was in a group of protesters at the nearby village of Nonwa. MOSOP was left to bury the dead and provide medicine for the wounded, including Mrs Korgbara.

The Ogoni people were traumatised by this event, and they protested on 30 April and the next day by massing on the roads and disrupting the movement of commuters. Some hoodlums attempted to vandalise Wilbros equipment.

The MOSOP Steering Committee was upset by this development and Mr Ledum Mitee, Edward Kobani and I were delegated to tour Ogoni to calm the people. Denied access to government radio, we sent letters appealing for calm to all villages through the chiefs. We followed that up the next day with visits to the two sensitive kingdoms of Gokan and

104

Tai, and the headquarters at Bori, where we spoke to large crowds, asking everyone to keep calm and maintain the peace. Calm was quickly restored.

In the face of this tragedy, some Ogoni politicians and traditional rulers, the friends of Governor Ada George, issued another press release which was given wide coverage in the newspaper and radio, castigating MOSOP and its leaders in the strongest terms over the shooting, denying their right to represent the Ogoni, and inviting the government to do whatever they wished in order to establish law and order to Ogoni. Their advertisement claimed to be on behalf of 'a very substantial section of the Ogoni leadership'.

Clearly, these advertisers were sponsored by the state government. Shell was later to use the advertisement in international circles in a vain attempt to show that MOSOP was working at cross-purposes with the Ogoni people, and that I, in particular, did not have the support of the Ogoni people.

Indeed, ever since February, when it was decided to monitor my activities, Shell had been working extraordinarily hard to destroy all my efforts. Now, do not ask me for hard evidence. These things are never done in writing, and even if it were done, neither of the parties would make the letters available to me. But Shell has accepted publicly that whenever it feels threatened in its operations, it appeals to the Federal authorities. At about this time Shell had decided not to work any more in Ogoni and had placed all its flow stations on automatic. The area, it claimed, was not safe for Shell staff.

I have to state that MOSOP did not stop Shell, although we did let it be known that the company was *persona non grata* in our land because of its destruction of the environment, its uncaring exploitation of the community, and its refusal to make any restitution whatsoever for the great harm it had done to the Ogoni people and environment.

In that sense, the Ogoni people will have lost nothing should Shell pull out of the area for ever. The company having taken over 900 million barrels of crude oil from the area in 35 years and put absolutely nothing back but death and degradation, the Ogoni people would be very foolish indeed to welcome it back without a full agreement, carefully worked out and signed. Serious questions of shortage of land and of sustainable development and the propensity of Federal Nigeria to exploit the Ogoni people in conjunction with the oil companies mean that the Ogoni people and their leaders must receive cast-iron guarantees before oil and gas can be mined in the area again. If this is not done, the Ogoni people will become extinct.

Shell feels affronted that a black man, a black community has dared to challenge it; and it has shown the world that the company is an environmental threat in Nigeria, but not in Europe or America. For this reason, it is determined to humiliate me publicly and to discredit the Ogoni people. It is, perhaps, a question of time and methods for them. Whatever does happen, I am pleased that the Ogoni people have been able to stand up to their denigration at the hands of Shell.

As to the advertisement by the self-proclaimed 'very substantial section of the Ogoni leadership', it annoyed the Ogoni people to a very high degree. The advertisement was meant to incite the government against the MOSOP. But MOSOP had not invited the people to protest against Wilbros and Shell. Women farmers had acted on their own, in response to a particular situation.

The sycophantic so-called leaders had libelled MOSOP and they knew it. They were deliberately using the government and its coercive instruments against MOSOP, its leaders and the Ogoni people. This led Edward Kobani to characterise them as 'vultures', a term which stuck for all time. Their action was in contradiction of the agreement reached at Beeri on 17 January 1993 after the first advertisement by the government-paid chiefs. They had succeeded in creating a breach between themselves (a tiny group) and the masses of the Ogoni people led by MOSOP. This breach was duly exploited by both the government and Shell.

By this time, Babangida and his cronies were churning out a decree, the infamous Treason and Treasonable Felony Decree 1993, which stipulated the death penalty for anyone who 'conspires with himself' to 'utter' the words 'ethnic autonomy' or plans secession or seeks to alter the boundaries of any local government or state previously decreed by the military authorities.

There was no doubt at whom the decree was aimed. Curiously, Shell's 'Briefing Note' issued at about the same time, and accusing me of seeking 'political self-determination' for the Ogoni people (as if that were a crime), agreed entirely with Babangida's law.

The Note, under the heading 'Tensions in Nigeria' protested that:

> 'Oil companies are being singled out for attention by activists because of increasing internal tensions in Nigeria. Local community concerns are being taken by international human rights groups and receiving media attention.'

It went on to claim that:

> 'Shell has been active in Nigeria for more than half a century. As operator for a joint venture in which it has a 30 per cent interest, Shell Petroleum Development Company (SPDC) has made a substantial contribution to the economic development of this large and complex African country. It has also contributed to community development.'

The Note outlines the background to the 'tensions', acknowledging openly that 'Oil, as Nigeria's main source of revenue, is a highly political subject'.

Unemployment is high among the rural communities in Nigeria, which includes most of the oil-producing areas. Young people, often highly educated, and other groups are frustrated, believing that these oil-producing areas in particular are not getting a fair share of the oil revenues, and are challenging traditional local leadership and government.

SPDC has sympathy for some of their concerns and played its part in persuading the Federal government to double the special fund for the development of the oil-producing areas from 1.5 to 3 per cent.

There is considerable doubt, however, as to how much, if any, of this money reached the people it was intended to help. New, more radical community leaders are emerging who, prevented by law from openly criticising the government, are targeting Shell.

Some demonstrations have been orderly, but others have been violent. In at least two incidents, protest led to police action which resulted in fatalities.

Shell, as by far the largest international oil company in Nigeria, is a convenient target for those seeking to internationalise the problem. A representative of the Ogoni people, Ken Saro-Wiwa, has been travelling abroad extensively. He has raised the profile of the issue with a number of activist groups, particularly in the Netherlands. Though he is attempting to single out the Ogonis for particular attention, their situation is no different from that of other oil-producing communities in Nigeria.

The Note goes on to deny the accusations, in particular that of gross environmental damage, insisting that:

Shell 'has conducted environmental impact studies on new developments in recent years, and has in place a five-year environmental plan for improving earlier and older installations'. The company also listed various community assistance programmes they had been running, even though 'community development is a government responsibility'.

'Despite the problems of recognising which claimants are

community leaders in times of change, SPDC is involved in discussions with Federal and state authorities and oil-producing and community leaders, including the Ogonis and Mr Saro-Wiwa.

However, Mr Saro-Wiwa has made his ultimate aims clear. He is seeking political 'self-determination' for the Ogoni people, for whom he says he is spokesman. Other Ogonis refute his claim and some only recently have resigned from his movement. Their claim for political self-determination and demands for US 10 billion dollars in royalties and reparation have been stated in his correspondence with overseas non-governmental organisations, Nigerian press reports and recently directly with SPDC.'

The Briefing Note ends:

Shell position

The reasons for Mr Saro-Wiwa's attacks on SPDC are therefore clear. He is attempting to use SPDC in his efforts to raise the international profile of his concerns for the Ogoni people and to meet his objective of their political self-determination. At no time has he acknowledged the positive contribution SPDC has made to Nigeria in its many forms. By involving SPDC in his emotive and exaggerated attacks, he wishes to gain the support of international pressure groups, whom he is personally visiting in many countries outside Nigeria with the objective of raising pressure on the Federal government of Nigeria.

Despite this, SPDC does sympathise with community concerns and continues to try in every possible way to help promote harmony between communities, local and Federal government and the oil companies working in these areas.

However, Shell believes that these are Nigerian problems. They should be resolved in Nigeria by agreement between Nigerian people.

* * *

Most of Shell's claims in this Briefing Note as they concern me and the Ogoni people are spurious and undignified. Shell's contribution to community development in Ogoni is negligible and is most insulting when quantified and placed side by side with what the company has taken out of the area or the harm it has caused the environment.

The roads allegedly built by Shell are often to its various locations, through farmland. They have the effect of depriving the Ogoni of much needed farmland and, strange as this may sound, force the poor farmers to wear shoes to their farms – a thing they can hardly afford. These so-called roads would not answer such exalted names in Europe.

In Ogoni, Shell locations lie pat in the middle of villages, in front and back gardens – and that should lay a particular responsibility on Shell to be absolutely cautious in its operations. The company, however, remains negligent and wilful. In the years from 1958 until MOSOP swung into action in 1993, Shell had no trouble whatsoever from the Ogoni people. But that is because the people were not organised, not because Shell was acting correctly. When the MOSOP gave voice to the voiceless, Shell persisted in its perverse ways, which had by then become habit. The double standards the company operated could be easily shown up. There were enough films, magazines and books to show how environmentally conscious Shell was in Europe and America. The story in Nigeria was entirely different.

Shell's behaviour in Europe and America was dictated by the pressure of environmental groups and the governments of the countries concerned. Given that, why did Shell take such great exception to my work and that of the MOSOP? I can only attribute it to the fact that Shell knows that the military dictatorships which have ruled or misruled Nigeria over the years have depended entirely on the revenue which Shell generates and are therefore beholden to the company in a very crucial manner. The company therefore adopts a godlike 'we can do no wrong' attitude.

To say that a community leader in Nigeria is prevented by law from openly criticising the government and therefore targets Shell is not true. Anyone who reads the newspapers in Nigeria will attest to the fact that no matter what laws are enacted, informed Nigerians openly criticise the government. Any of my books and numerous newspaper essays will bear testimony to my wide-ranging, strident and scathing criticism of government. My criticism of Shell was in the same tradition.

Indeed, most of the top Nigerian employees of Shell happen to have been my contemporaries at school and university. Some of them have told me privately that they agree with most of the points I have made, and that they have raised the same points only to find that they cannot influence company policy, which is invariably dictated from The Hague or London.

I challenge Shell to show the public what environmental impact assessment it conducted in Nigeria prior to 1993. To accuse me of 'emotive and exaggerated attacks' is to attempt to deflect attention from my criticisms of Shell's environmental record. It is cheap propaganda and deserves to be dismissed contemptuously.

It is well known that a boil on one's nose is more painful to the afflicted than an earthquake which happens thousands of miles away killing thousands of people. I am inclined to think that this is why the Ogoni environment must matter more to me than Shell International ensconced in its ornate offices on the banks of the Thames in London. But I cannot allow the company its smugness because its London comfort spells death to my Ogoni children and compatriots.

I am flattered that Shell should find me deserving of so much attention. However, they are going after the messenger instead of the message. And there is no doubt in my mind that they are on the wrong path and that they will finally admit the truth and thank me for enabling them to create a healthy operational environment in which they can reap the profits which I do not begrudge them. I can only hope that they will not have entirely ruined the Ogoni people by their present obtuseness before that time comes.

I should stress that Shell either completely and deliberately misunderstands my intentions, or puts a wrong construction on them for its own mischievous purposes. Let me state here, for the avoidance of all doubt, that my overall concern is for the fragile ecosystem of the Niger Delta – one of the richest areas on earth. I am appalled that this rich company, with the abundance of knowledge and material resources available to it, should treat the area with such callous indifference. I consider the loss of the Niger Delta a loss to all mankind and therefore regard Shell's despoliation of the area as a crime to all humanity.

Ogoni is but a thousand of the 70,000 kilometres of the Niger River Delta. If I have predicated my struggle for the delta environment on Ogoni and the Ogoni people, it is only because I recognise that the argument is an arduous, dangerous and expensive one. Ogoni is a good laboratory to make the experiments which will apply to the delta as a whole. My methodology is scientific. Besides, my political argument is predicated on ethnic self-reliance. The delta is host to about 20 different people and cultures. The success of the Ogoni is bound to influence all the others positively in the same direction – and, by implication, the rest of Nigeria. Thus, Shell errs and misunderstands me woefully when it seeks to categorise my endeavours as some localised action by a self-proclaimed 'spokesman' of the Ogoni people.

I am aware that Shell often prefers to deal with its problems secretly and outside of the public purview. Unfortunately, where the Niger River Delta (and Ogoni) environment is concerned, the issue is public because the neglect of the past is of enormous proportions and remediation will be expensive. Shell's shareholders might well need to know in advance what their Nigerian operations are going to cost their pocketbooks.

The amount of compensation demanded by the Ogoni people is peanuts and this shall be proved when an environmental audit is done to determine how much damage Shell has done. If one spill from the *Exxon Valdez* could cost Exxon five billion dollars in punitive damages, Shell must pay more than the four billion dollars which the Ogoni have demanded in reparation for the ecological damage to the people and the land over a 35-year period in which there have been spills, blow-outs and continual gas flaring.

Besides, Shell knows that royalty is, by definition, what is paid to a landlord for minerals extracted from his land. When Shell pays 20 per cent in royalties and rents to the Nigerian government, and turns round and thumps its chest because it has encouraged the government to pay the landlords 3 per cent instead of 20, then there must be something really wrong with the policy of the company.

Shell knows, for instance, how much it pays the Shetlands Council in the UK annually in taxes, just for siting oil tanks in Sullum Voe. Knowing how much it pays, by comparison, to the Ogoni local government councils, the company should be ashamed to join issues with the Ogoni people on this matter.

The good thing is that the Ogoni people now know and will no longer be taken on a ride by Shell. No matter how hard the company tries to wriggle out of it, they will have to confront the truth of their Ogoni operations soon. And then, they will find that indifference and double standards are expensive items for a multinational interested in world-wide operations. Shell must compensate the Ogoni people fully for their losses.

Shell should adopt the path of dialogue. MOSOP has left its doors open for such dialogue. In the interest of both parties.

But to return to my story, on the night of 4 May I tuned in, fortuitously, to the 11 o'clock news summary on Nigerian television. And I heard the Federal Attorney-General Minister of Justice Mr Clement Akpambo say in reply to a question as to whether the decree was aimed at me and the Ogoni people, that if the cap fitted, we should wear it. A few days later we received a call to make another visit to Abuja.

On the first occasion, as I have related, the Director-General of the SSS, Mr Peter Ndiokwu, had read us the riot act, and we had asked for justice and understanding.

When next we visited, Mr Ndiokwu asked that we should allow Shell to lay its pipeline in Ogoni. We could not promise that. When he mentioned that my writing could get me into detention. I told him that detention only makes writers stronger.

On the occasion of our third visit in early May, we were accompanied by Albert Badey, who had begun to attend the meetings of the Steering Committee of the MOSOP. The first man to raise doubts as to his presence at our meetings was Edward Kobani, who expressed reservations privately to me of Albert's good faith. He said the he knew for a fact that Albert was meeting regularly with the group that had denounced MOSOP publicly after the shooting at the end of April.

But I assured him that I thought Albert's talents would be very useful to the committee. I truly thought that Edward was merely transferring the rivalry of Bodo, their common home place, where divisions were deep and complicated, to the committee, and I was not going to allow that to happen. With the twenty-twenty vision of hindsight, I now realise that I was wrong. Albert's mission was to disrupt the MOSOP. Who sent him remains a mystery to me.

Our third trip to Abuja brought us face to face with the power behind the throne: Brigadier-General Halilu Akilu, head of the National Intelligence Agency; Major-General Aliyu Mohammed, National Security Adviser; Alhaji Aliyu Mohammed, Secretary General to the Federal military government. Speaking with them at the glittering presidential palace, I had the feeling that Big Brother was listening in on a hidden television screen.

The discussion went quite well. Major-General Aliyu Mohammed is a very genial man, and General Aliyu showed sympathy for our cause, as did Akilu. They expressed surprise when we showed them the ethnic make-up of Rivers State. It became clear to them that we were also being oppressed at state level. I believe that they had initially thought that all people from Rivers State were one.

They gave the impression that they wanted to do something and asked that we provide a list of all unemployed Ogoni youths and information on how oil-bearing areas in other parts of the country are treated by their governments. They also asked that we indicate once again in writing precisely what we wanted.

When we returned to Port Harcourt, a delegation was sent by the MOSOP Steering Committee to Governor Ada George to complain about the silence of his government on the shootings that had occurred in Biara. The delegation consisted of the elderly members of the committee along with Ledum Mitee.

The delegation returned to inform us that upon the pleas of Governor Ada George, who apparently went on his knees to them, they had agreed to allow Shell to lay its pipelines and accept compensation for the wounded and the dead of the Biara incident.

The Steering Committee members were angry at this, as the delegation did not have the mandate to come to a decision on its behalf, or on behalf of the Ogoni people. The deal was rejected outright. And the gerontocrats were furious. Their reputations, they argued, were at stake. Whose fault we asked them? Here was another sign of trouble.

The first sign had occurred when Babangida, in one of his famous U-turns, suddenly lifted the ban on old politicians and both Edward Kobani and Dr Leton became free to take part in party politics. We had agreed that in the interest of MOSOP, none of its top officials should do so, as that would leave them open to partisanship and divide the members of the movement.

In defiance of the agreement, Edward Kobani decided to contest the post of Chairman of the Rivers State branch of the Social Democratic Party. Luckily for us, he crashed, beaten by a chap young enough to be his son. It was a disgrace which he might have avoided.

Then, Dr Leton, also in defiance of our agreement, decided that he would become a delegate to the National Convention of the Social Democratic Party. He had already won a delegate seat before we became aware of what he was up to. At a meeting of the Steering Committee, the danger to MOSOP of what this meant was brought to his notice. He gave the impression that he would comply with our wishes and stand down. He reneged on his word and duly attended the convention.

At this stage, our advice was to get both of them voted out of their positions as Vice-President and President respectively, which the Steering Committee would surely have done. But on consideration of the danger of tearing the movement apart, we decided to leave them in their positions. This was an error. Both men were becoming a liability, and their decision to allow the construction of the Shell pipeline against the desire of the Steering Committee was adding to our burdens.

I had to travel to London for family reasons and went off in the middle of May. My passport was confiscated at the airport, and I missed the flight on which I had been booked. A midnight phone call to Major-General Aliyu Mohammed, the National Security Advisor, ensured that I retrieved the passport and enabled me to travel the following night.

On arrival in London, the Secretariat of UNPO at The Hague felt that in view of the Treason and Treasonable Felony Decree 1993 which hung on my neck like a millstone, I should travel to make objections to the decree known in Europe. I met with Foreign Office desk officers of the United Nations Human Rights Commission and the International Commission of Jurists in Geneva. This was, as expected, transmitted to Abuja. The men in power did not like it. I also gave an interview to CNN which, I guess, did not please Abuja either.

Before I could return to Nigeria, news came that Dr Leton, Edward Kobani and Albert Badey were doing all in their power to convince the Ogoni people to allow the construction of the Shell pipeline to proceed. I made my objections known to them, sending an emissary from my Lagos office to deliver a personal message to them. As fate would have it, the local people would not hear of the completion of the pipeline either.

I returned to Port Harcourt at the beginning of June, 10 days or so before the presidential elections scheduled for 12 June. As early as February I had mooted the idea of our having to boycott the elections in pursuance of the non-violent struggle for our rights. The idea had been well received by several members of the Steering Committee, the party politicians excepted. Dr Bennet Birabi had spent almost an hour on the telephone from Abuja to me in London on 29 May to convince me that an election boycott would not be in *his* political interests. I advised him to come to the next MOSOP Steering Committee meeting, where the matter would be discussed.

A meeting of the Committee was scheduled for 2 June, the day after my arrival. Both 1 and 2 June were Muslim holidays and I did not meet any of the members of the Committee before the meeting, which took place as usual in the residence of Dr Leton.

I placed before the meeting a motion that we boycott the elections. The motion was hotly debated, and in the end Dr Leton as Chairman decided, after pressure from Edward Kobani, to put it to the vote. The boycotters won by 11 votes to six. Kobani immediately gave notice that he would not accept the majority decision, even if he had to resign as Vice-President.

Two days later, I was in my Aggrey Road office in the morning when in trooped Dr Leton, Edward Kobani, Albert Badey, Titus Nwieke, who was Treasurer of MOSOP, and Engineer Apenu. Their purpose was to convince me to rescind the decision of the Steering Committee to boycott the elections. I did not see my way through that, and told them so. A democratic decision had been taken and it was our responsibility to carry it out. They left my office after a hot exchange, as angry as they could be. Both Dr Leton and Edward Kobani informed me that they would be resigning. It was up to them, I said, and there rested the matter.

I was due to travel to Vienna to attend the United Nations World Conference on Human Rights scheduled for 11 June. Before leaving for Lagos, en route to Vienna, I travelled through Ogoni to place before the people the decision of the Steering Committee to boycott the presidential elections. Everywhere I went, the decision was applauded and upheld. At each place I advised that there was to be no violence on Election Day, and that those who wanted to vote should not be obstructed from doing so. I expected that the turn-out for the election would help us decide the popularity or otherwise of MOSOP.

I held a press conference as 'spokesman' of the Ogoni people to explain to the nation why we would be boycotting the elections. I explained, firstly, that the constitution of the Federal Republic of Nigeria (1989) discriminates against the Ogoni people as an oil-producing section of the country, expropriates their land and resources, does not protect them as a minority of 500,000 people in a country of 80 million, and consigns them to extinction.

Secondly, I pointed out that the political structure designed by the departing military and inserted by them into the constitution condemns the Ogoni to second-class citizenship and denies them their fundamental human rights to self-determination – rights which are enjoyed by other Nigerians.

The 1989 constitution was not subjected to a referendum and the methods of the constituent assembly were, to say the least, inimical to democracy.

Since the election of 12 June will produce a President who will swear to protect the diseased and undemocratic constitution of 1989, the Ogoni have decided that to vote in that election will be a vote for slavery, genocide and extinction.

The Ogoni people demand the immediate convening of a sovereign national conference to discuss reforms of the existing political constitutional system and to redress the balance of power in the country so that ethnic minorities in the nation-state can exercise all those rights conferred by the African Charter of Human and Peoples Rights and the United Nations Bill of Rights to which Nigeria is a signatory.

I went off to Lagos on 7 June to complete arrangements to enable me travel to Vienna. Delay in receipt of my airline ticket kept me in Lagos longer than expected. During that time I got a telephone call informing me that the radio in Port Harcourt had been announcing, in my name, that the Ogoni people would vote in the elections, contrary to the decisions that had been taken by the MOSOP Steering Committee and approved by the people. I issued a prompt denial.

In any case, the activists on the ground had not been deceived by the announcement, which they knew to be a dirty trick. They therefore went into action in Ogoni to ensure that the trick did not succeed and that the people were not deceived.

I was to come to learn later, while in police custody at Owerri, that the Ogoni party politicians, including Dr Leton, Edward Kobani and Bennet Birabi, had met and resolved to make the public announcement in my name. It was essentially a forgery. And, believe it or not, Dr Leton told me about it with a straight face, in the presence of an inspector of police, Mr Ledum Mitee, Dr Birabi and Mr Simeon Idemyor, my cousin. Dr Birabi had written my name in his own hand beneath the announcement.

I have to state that I was shocked beyond belief by Dr Leton's revelation of the trick. I had a very high opinion of him. I had met him first at the University of Nigeria, where he was a graduate assistant a few months before the outbreak of the Nigerian civil war. A big man, handsome, well built and highly intelligent, he stuck me at the time as the quintessential Ogoni man. He had studied at the Methodist Boys High School, Oron, and the Hope Waddell Training Institute before he proceeded to the University of London to take his First and a doctorate in chemistry.

For all his education, he was very much wedded to Ogoni culture. He could sing and dance traditional Ogoni songs in a way which few of the educated élite in Ogoni could ever equal. And he won my heart.

Garrick Leton would shine wherever he might be. He often joked that he was not a politician, but liked to profit by politics. For all that, I did feel that he was politically naïve. An honest man, but I often thought he was not in tune with Nigerian politics, and that he was probably not meant for that life. I often wished that he had remained within academia.

As he confirmed the dirty trick that had been played on the Ogoni people that day, I wept inwardly for him, and for Bennet Birabi on whom I had invested so much emotion and my lean resources at an earlier time.

But to get back to my story, on the night of 11 June I was on my way to Vienna to attend the United Nations Human Rights Conference, when my passport was again confiscated at the airport and I was not able to travel. I had, however, sent the materials for a planned photographic exhibition of the environmental degradation of Ogoni in advance and other Ogoni activists, including Ledum Mitee, did travel to Vienna. So all was well from an Ogoni point of view. I resented the denial of my rights, of course, but that could wait. The Vienna Conference was useful to the Ogoni because Ledum Mitee met Anita Roddick there, thanks to the UNPO. Anita Roddick and her organisation, The Body Shop, were later to play a very important role in the Ogoni struggle.

I was in Lagos on 12 June and was by the television at night to hear of the boycott of the elections in Ogoni and of a minor fracas involving Dr Bennet Birabi.

Apparently, on the morning of the elections, finding that even the people in his hometown, Yeghe, had resolved not to vote, Bennet summoned them to the town square and publicly berated them. The answer of the people was that he hadn't spoken to them since he won his last election. And they wondered why he would get them together only because an election from which he hoped to benefit was due. In effect, they gave him notice that they were not prepared to be exploited politically, not even by a local politician. The meeting ended in a public disgrace for Bennet, who was, at the time, the Senate Minority Leader. But the people weren't finished with him. Just in case, in the usual dishonest manner of the Nigerian politician, ballot boxes were being stuffed in his house, some of his own relations went to his home to check. And that is where one of his aides sustained a minor injury.

I also learned that Ogoni youths in various locations physically stopped the movement of ballot boxes; and also of some politicians, such as Edward Kobani, who were forced to remain indoors through the period of voting. Some young men even stopped election materials from being delivered by the Electoral Commission, turning back vehicles which carried such materials.

All of which I very much regret, since this is not the sort of boycott we had envisaged. But the fault must be put squarely at the door of all those politicians who conspired to forge my signature on a document to which I was not privy, hoping thus to use the confidence which the Ogoni people have in my leadership for their own benefit. I have sued the radio station and all those involved in the forgery, since the police have refused to act on the complaints made to them about it. The refusal of the Ogoni people to be exploited by their politicians indicates the success of our mobilisation efforts and the political education of the Ogoni people. The Ogoni people have always known what was right, but sometimes lacked the leadership that would encourage them to stick by it. What MOSOP had done was to empower them.

The next day, Sunday 13 June, Nigeria's national news-papers were full of news of the Ogoni boycott. The Ogoni had made the point that they would not accept slavery and extinc-tion, or for that matter the legalisation of the expropriation of their resources, which is what the constitution (under which the elections were being held) stipulated.

I was as proud as a peacock that Sunday. I felt that no matter what happened, the Ogoni people had redeemed themselves. At long last!

Chapter Seven

THE success, so far, of the non-violent struggle of the Ogoni people led me, invariably, to think of the possible implications for the rest of Nigeria and, indeed, for black Africa. For the continent is made up of nation-states conceived in the European colonialist interest for imperial or commercial purposes. In virtually every nation-state there are several 'Ogonis' – despairing and disappearing people suffering the yoke of political marginalisation, economic strangulation and environmental degradation, or a combination of these, unable to lift a finger to save themselves. What is their future?

In 1844 European powers had gathered in Berlin to carve up the African continent along water courses and lines of longitude on a map. I have often pictured to myself the scene at conference table where it all happened, and ground my teeth at the little realised consequences of the actions of the conferees on the unsuspecting African peoples and nations, the victims of that exercise. People got separated willy-nilly, coming under the different administrations of different European nations; old African empires were destroyed in the new structures which resulted from the misadventure, and several cultures were henceforth forced to live under the same roof, so to speak.

The partition of Africa was to be followed by the pacification of the people who either dared to protest the new imposition or had to be brought under the new colonial administration. In the heyday of the idea of the nation-state in

Europe, new African nation-states came into being. European will, European desires were always the underlying factors. The pacification exercise meant the destruction of peoples, of ways of life; and it took different forms in different regions of black Africa.

I do not suggest the colonial experience was only destructive. It may well have enhanced and improved some people, freeing them from local tyrannies and offering them new opportunities. However, the overall effect is there for us to see today, as African nation-states reel under the seemingly insoluble political and economic burdens.

The African nation-state owed its continued existence under colonial rule to the coercion of the colonising power. In the case of Nigeria, about 200 different people and cultures whose major link is skin colour were brought together under a single administration for the first time in 1914. Under colonial rule, the clash of people was controlled by administrative fiat. Well, not quite: the clash of cultures remained an undercurrent while colonial rule lasted and afterwards. With the advent of political independence in the 1960s, the clash of peoples and cultures moved into a more prominent position. It could only be controlled by the use of coercive force, which the new élite which inherited the colonial mantle readily used. This explains the prevalence on the continent of military dictatorships or civilian dictatorships bolstered by armies bequeathed by the departing European colonialists.

The experience of the Ogoni people in the twentieth century, briefly put, is a tale of administrative neglect, of exploitation and slavery in which the British colonial administration, the newly emergent Nigerian nation-state, the rules thereof and signally, the multi-national oil giant Shell have had a role to play. The Ogoni have, themselves, unwittingly lent a hand to their denigration, as is usual among indigenous people on the way to extinction.

The Ogoni first came into contact with the British in 1901. A column of armed African men under the command of a young British officer raiding Ogoni villages sporadically between 1908 and 1913 was enough to 'pacify' the Ogoni and to destroy the social fabric of their society. The Ogoni were absorbed into the Nigerian nation-state in 1914. Thereafter, the British administrator, billeted hundreds of miles away, did not bother to establish anything whatsoever in Ogoni, except that an Irish missionary, belonging to the Primitive Methodist Mission, began to work among the Ogoni and was soon followed by African missionaries of their religious denominations.

Twenty-five years after their first arrival, the local British administrators were conscience-stricken by their neglect of 'this large tribe' and sent in the lone British administrator (District Officer) who began to get the Ogoni to cut roads, build court houses and pay their taxes to a central, local administration. Even then, the effort was half-hearted. The Ogoni did not benefit from any infusion of funds from outside, and it was to take all of nearly 50 years before the Ogoni, in 1947, were able to get an administration called 'Native Authority' devoted entirely to their own affairs. Thenceforth, their taxes could be devoted solely to their development, overseen by their chiefs and elders. Alas, too late! Constitutional developments in the wider Nigerian nation of which they were only a nominal part had left them far behind. They found themselves in an administrative set-up, a 'region', called Eastern Nigeria – one of the three regions into which Nigeria had been carved in 1951. By 1956, the Native Authority system was duly scrapped and the Ogoni had less than 10 years of some form of limited autonomy in which they could do things for themselves.

Everything happened to the Ogoni: colonisation, pacification, absorption into Nigeria, allocation into Eastern Nigeria. And more was to come, none more important than the arrival of the drilling gigs of Shell in 1956, and the commencement of oil production and pollution in 1958. Then, in 1960, Nigerian independence.

As Nigeria celebrated independence, the Ogoni were consigned to political slavery at the hands of the new black colonialists wearing the mask of Nigerianism. The new Nigerian masquerade was in the public arena, leashed to a rope held by an unseen hand, and steadied by the oil of the Ogoni and other peoples in the Niger River Delta. In effect, the producers of that oil, the multinational oil giants, truly controlled the masquerade in the arena. And if any child dared do more than enjoy the dance of the masquerade, it was liable to be frightened to death by it.

The image of the masquerade dancing in a public arena is one which an African can relate to quite easily. In the masquerade is a man, an ordinary human being subject to the usual humours which afflict humanity. Yet, once he wears a mask, he is transformed into something else, something dangerous. The masquerade can perpetrate evil, hurt spectators. And that is why, when a masquerade engages in more than its share of evil, brave spectators are allowed to disrobe it. The mask falls from its wearer and the puny man in the masquerade is seen for what he truly is: all flesh and blood, the son of so-and-so. This unmasking of the cruel masquerade is very important. But it is a difficult task.

By 1966, six years after the attainment of independence, the Nigerian masquerade was running amok in the public arena. The clash of cultures and peoples was leading to catastrophe. The three biggest ethnic groups in Nigeria, the Hausa, the Igbo and the Yoruba, were at each other's throats. The oil of the Ogoni and other small ethnic nations in the Niger Delta fuelled the feud and, predictably, the Ogoni were to suffer as grass in the fight of two elephants. In the civil war which raged between 1967 and 1979, an estimated 30,000 Ogoni people, about 10 per cent of the population, died, most of them in the refugee camps in the Igbo heartland to which they had been forcibly evacuated on the orders of Ojukwu, the Igbo warlord.

One result of the war for the Ogoni is that they were now grouped into a Rivers State (Nigeria having been split into 12 states as a way to blunt the Biafran secessionist threat). Within the context of Rivers State, the Ogoni could make much more progress than was possible in an asphyxiating Eastern Nigeria, with its massive, all-powerful Igbo majority. Some Ogoni did manage to acquire an education and to begin to function within the Nigerian nation in a limited way. But Nigeria was headed in the wrong direction. The nation was not about to care for its minority ethnic groups, or to allow the producers of oil to enjoy the benefits thereof. It was to remain a slave society in which jungle law predominated, allowing survival only to the fittest, the more numerous groups. And the men who controlled the means of violence, the military bosses, were headed for the spoils of war: the rich oil-find in the Niger Delta.

By 1990 the Nigerian masquerade had become a real pain to the Ogonis, the more painful because Ogoni resources had gone to dress it up. And in the masquerade were bungling soldiers who mounted platitudes about Nigerian unity and all such, while they purloined the Ogoni and others.

It had become painfully clear, after 30 years of independence, that the main thing which bound the various ethnic groups consisting the Nigerian nation was skin colour, apart from the commercial interests of the erstwhile colonial master. And skin colour is not strong enough to stop the oppression of one group by another. Sometimes it reinforces oppression because it makes it less obvious. White people oppressing blacks in South Africa draws instant condemnation because it is seen to be racial. But black upon black oppression merely makes people shrug and say, 'Well, it's their business, isn't it?'

No one could hope to disrobe the masquerade without finding out the views of those who held its leash. Accordingly, I found time to brief the British High Commissioner in Lagos on my views and on what I purposed to do. Shell in Nigeria is controlled by the British arm of the multinational, although it is not really as simple as that; Shell's organisation is as complex and convoluted as they come. But it is enough that some recent Managing Directors of Shell Nigeria have risen to become Managing Director and Chief Executive of Shell International based in London. Nigeria produces 14 per cent of Shell's total oil output. Shell's profit from its Nigerian operations is said to be very high, which should surprise no-one. Shell does not spend as much on environmental protection, salaries and health care as it does in other countries where the company operates. So, indeed, Shell matters a great deal to the British government. And Shell's Nigerian operations tie in neatly with the British government's overwhelming interest in Africa's largest nation and market, its former colony.

My contact with the British High Commission and subsequently with the Foreign and Commonwealth Office in London was minimal, exploratory – but it was enough to enable me to form the impression that there was a mind-set about Nigeria. Stability seemed to be their credo; stability to ensure continued economic 'co-operation', for which read exploitation. In that sense, the Ogoni argument was a minor irritant. Nor did it have a chance of success unless it was backed by – wait for it – Shell. But in fairness to those I met, I should say that they listened patiently, and pointed me to that other great institution of the British: the liberal lobby. This was how I came into contact with the Parliamentary Human Rights Group headed by Lord Avebury, and thence to other non-governmental organisations interested in human rights.

As with the British, so with the Dutch and the Swiss whom I had the opportunity to meet on one or two occasions in their home offices. They were even further removed from the problem, the Dutch interest being pre-eminently connected with Shell. In effect, the problems of Nigeria, of Africa, were not really on the table. The tribal problems that were important were those of the disintegrated Soviet Union or of Yugoslavia. Europe itself had sorted out its tribal problems much earlier and was now dedicated to supervising other people's, ensuring that there was enough stability all round to allow the business of economic exploitation for European comfort to proceed apace.

No, there would not be help for the Ogoni from European officialdom, until there was a radical change of government policy. The danger was that a change of government might move in a direction opposite to what I was proposing, based on my experience of Nigerian life. As William Ptaff asserts, it is now the convention in right-thinking Western circles that Africa's tribes and ethnic groups are repressive colonial inventions and that nothing significant distinguishes Zulu from Xhosa, Masai from Kikuyu, or Tutsi from Hutu, notwithstanding the reactionary Western sciences of ethnology and anthropology. Right thinking! What absolute balderdash. Even more unforgivable is Ali Mazrui, whose very sharp intellect lets him down when he proposes the re-establishment of the old League of Nations trusteeship system, with African and Asian nations among those appointed by the United Nations to govern certain countries under the guidance of a council of major African states which would possess a peace-keeping army. Again, an army. And 'major African states' such as Nigeria, no doubt. Perish the thought.

Robert Heilbroner, in his book *The Future as History: The Historic Currents of our Time and the Directions in which They are Taking America (1960),* says:

imperialism imposed on its colonies the raw economic drive of capitalism without the social political underpinnings and protections which blunted that drive home . . . Into [the] primitive circulation of life a powerful and dangerous virus was injected with terrible effect. It turned millions of traditionally self-sufficient peasants into rubber-tappers, coffee-growers, tin miners, tea-pickers – and then subjected this new agricultural mining proletariat to the incomprehensible vagaries of world commodity fluctuations. It uprooted ancient laws and gave in exchange Western justice, whose ideas disrupted the local culture by striking at the root of time-honoured traditions and customs...Colonialism, even in its most missionary moments, never succeeded in seeing the 'natives' as equals, and it usually took for granted their irremediable inferiority.

Well said, in general. Applied to the Ogoni, we should say British imperialism imposed on them oil exploitation and the Nigerian nation-state, both powerful and dangerous forces which together spelt omnicide in Ogoni.

I do not think that the remedy for what Robert Heilbroner describes is a return to Europe or United Nations colonialism. Based on my experience of Ogoni life, I can confidently say that it is still possible to return to 'the local culture': in short, to re-create societies, which have been destroyed by European colonialism, neo-colonialism, or the newly inspired and even more destructive 'black colonialism'. And what we need to do is examine each society critically, identify the motive spirit of its being and mobilise its people to new horizons.

I do not think that there is any ethnic group in Nigeria which cannot survive on its own. Far from being 'repressive colonial inventions', Africa's tribes and ethnic groups are ancient and enduring social organisations complete with their own mores and visions, which no colonialism has been able to destroy over the centuries. The African nation-state as presently conceived, has only succeeded in stultifying them, in denying them their vital force and limiting their capacity for self-reliance.

The men who argued for Nigerian independence, and particularly Obafemi Awolowo, clearly knew the foregoing and argued convincingly that the only way forward for Nigeria was to allow each ethnic group to exercise autonomy and grow at its own pace using its genius and its political system. The British colonialists rather than allow this, created a federation of 'regions', each region being run as a unitary state. Thus, there was 'unitarism' at regional level and 'federalism' at the centre. This predictably came to grief, because in the regions there were ethnic groups struggling for autonomy, while at the centre the regions fought each other for control of the commonwealth of Nigeria. When this resulted in disastrous civil war, an attempt was made, through the creation of states, to return to a proper federation of ethnic groups. Had this process been carried to its logical conclusion Nigeria might have seen progress. However, the Nigerian military foolishly turned back the hands of the clock and returned Nigeria to a *de facto* unitary state, while proclaiming the nation still a federation. The state creation exercise was soon turned into an instrument of internal colonialism. The Hausa was split into eight states, The Yoruba into six, and the Igbo into four. Meanwhile, the smaller ethnic groups were herded into unitary states, where they continue to suffer political and social discrimination. Thus, a group like the Ogoni, rich and viable as a unit, capable of practising self-reliance, find themselves in Rivers State, where they have to scramble for survival with nine other ethnic groups who are together marginalised by the Nigerian centre.

When I started MOSOP, one of my purposes was to draw attention to this unholy alliance between oil interests and the Nigerian military, which enforces military or even civilian dictatorships over Nigerian democracy as well as the vital force of Nigerian federalism and individual Nigerian ethnic groups.

I was aware of the success, in the past, of the mobilisation movements which had been based on the ethnic group. In the1950s, Dr Nnamdi Azikiwe had successfully mobilised the Igbo, Chief Obafemi Awolowo the Yoruba, Ahmadu Bello the Hausa-Fulani and Tarka the Tiv. This mobilisation effort had not been stopped by the British. It had, indeed, brought Nigerian independence sooner rather than later.

Unfortunately for the Ogoni, their mobilisation was being opposed by the military dictatorship in Nigeria and their allies. Whether we would succeed was still to be seen.

Should the Ogoni movement succeed, it will point a way for the rest of Nigeria, if not Africa. While I agree that the borders imposed by 1884 Berlin are not perfect, I am not anxious at this time to re-draw them. I believe that the nation-states as they currently stand can be allowed to exist, but within them there must be the practice of federalism based on ethnic groups. Each ethnic group must be mobilised and taught to be self-reliant. And each must be allowed to grow at its own pace, politically and economically. Each must be allowed to control its environment and economy. Hence, as I have said previously, I call for the practice of ERECTISM – Ethnic Autonomy, Resource and Environmental Control – within each nation-state which must be run as a federation. This is the way forward for Africa. But will Europe and the multinationals who control Africa's wealth allow it? Because that would mean progress for Africa, and I am still to be convinced that the West and their multinational corporations want African progress. They want Africa to remain at their feet. It seems to me that only the liberals in the West want African progress, and they aren't in power.

It has been asked in Nigeria if we could have successfully mobilised the Ogoni if there had not been oil, a devastated environment which would win world attention, and a small, easily organised population. My answer is that where there is a will, there is a way. Indeed, the presence of oil and a devastated environment have made the task of mobilisation even more difficult. These twin evils have drawn the ire of the Nigerian military dictatorship upon the Ogoni. Dividing the Ogoni, overtly and covertly, the better to be able to rule them, has become a credo. And this is what threatens to destroy the Ogoni movement. Had these elements been absent, mobilisation would have been much easier, more effective. All it would have needed is a leader (who will always emerge) capable of pointing a people to their ability to survive in the past, and the need for survival in the future. Oil pointed to the possibility of economic viability but we were always aware that brains are more important than mineral resources.

Certainly, what we have done for the Ogoni can be done for

other groups in Nigeria, in Africa. Its importance lies in the fact that a small ethnic group has not only been prepared psychologically to confront its history and take its fortune into its own hands, but is prepared to take on its oppressors in the form of the nation-state and multinational giant.

It is also very important that we have chosen the path of non-violent struggle. Our opponents are given to violence and we cannot meet them on their turf, even if we wanted to. Non-violent struggle offers weak people the strength which they otherwise would not have. The spirit becomes important, and no gun can silence that. I am aware, though, that non-violent struggle occasions more death than armed struggle. And that remains a cause for worry at all times. Whether the Ogoni people will be able to withstand the rigours of the struggle is yet to be seen. Their ability to do so will point the way of peaceful struggle to other peoples on the African continent.

Chapter Eight

So much for the thoughts which ran through my mind as I waited in the detention cell of the Nigerian Police at Owerri. One week had gone, and our captors had still not returned; nor was there word as to what that would happen.

I instructed Barry Kumbe to go to court to demand our release. He went to work immediately but was making no progress. No judge in Rivers State was willing to sign writs. Wherever Barry went in the state, he was told that there had been a red alert on me and all cases related to me. Of course, we might have pursued the case which we had filed in Lagos. But the Lagos courts were not sitting, since all Lagos lawyers had decided that they would boycott the law courts in protest against the annulment of the 12 June elections. What to do?

Barry decided to file the case in Owerri where we were being held. There, he had no problems whatsoever and the hearing was fixed for early July, by which time we would have been in detention for almost 10 days. At this time, Ledum Mitee was away in Vienna, where he had gone to attend the United Nations World Human Rights Conference.

Our captors returned a week and a day after we had been in Owerri. The presence of Mr Ogbeifun and his man Friday had not yet started to give me a running stomach. When he came in that afternoon, I still thought that he was doing a job for which he had some distaste. At that moment, I had in the cell Bishop Poromon, the Methodist Bishop of Port Harcourt, an

Ogoni man. There were others with him, including Mina my friend who had brought me food, and my personal assistant, Mr Deebi Nwiado, who had come to brief me on his journey to Vienna.

No sooner did Mr Ogbeifun come in than he started to bully me. Why were there others in the cell? Well, he could tolerate the presence of the man of God, but the rest, goodness, he could not, would not tolerate. Was I asking that I be sent to where I really belonged: the cramped guardroom downstairs where all the suspects were meant to be kept?

Bishop Poromon, a man of few words and great courtesy, was astounded. He offered to say a prayer. Mr Ogbeifun gruffly allowed him to do so. And he prayed for me, my fellow captives and our captors. And then he graciously withdrew.

When we were left alone, Mr Ogbeifun grabbed all the papers I had on the writing-table and went through them. Among them was a diary of my first week in detention, some papers from the Vienna Conference, and poems which I had begun to write. He warned that I did not have the right to write, and if I was not on good behaviour, he would have no option but to treat me according to the book.

To bring the enormity of my crime to me, he ordered that Dube and Nwiee be sent to the guardroom downstairs. He had me cheap there, because I would rather have gone down with them than allow them to go there alone. For my peace of mind, and against my instincts, I had to appeal to him to let us stay together in the wretched room to which we had been consigned.

Having thus humiliated me, he now casually informed me that he still had no further orders from his superiors and that he would have to return me to Lagos. We would have to wait in Owerri.

I raised the matter of my health with him, arguing that I ought really to be in hospital, if my condition was not to further deteriorate. I asked him to have a word with Dr Idoko, if he wanted to have confirmation. I was to learn later that Mr

Ogbeifun could not do anything without the approval of his superior in Lagos, the Deputy Inspector-General of Police in charge of the FIIB.

As I watched Mr Ogbeifun and his man Friday walk off that evening – it was about 6.30 pm – I remembered what my brother told me at the Central Police Station in Port Harcourt: that I would be away for a long time. It didn't sound funny this time.

Once I accepted that I might be in detention for an indefinite period, I ceased to worry about what orders came from Lagos. Mr Ogbeifun and his superiors could go hang. And as for the man with the ultimate responsibility for our detention, General Ibrahim Babangida, I reserved for him that contempt which I normally accord to vermin. I settled into my new life in a proper frame of mind. The only worry I had was my health, about which I could do precious little anyway.

The days were not particularly dull, come to face it. I had the use of my transistor radio and bought newspapers daily, so I was well informed. I was also able to read whatever book I wanted. I have to state that the police officers and men at the station were kind and polite to us. There was absolutely no hostility towards me, Dube and Nwiee, and where we needed anything, they exerted themselves to help.

One of the senior police officers had served with an Ogoni man in his early days in the force, and he had not forgotten what times they shared. On that score alone, he became a frequent visitor to our cell and was quite solicitous of our comfort. He made sure that my supply of pipe tobacco did not run out.

Journalism also kept me occupied. They would come into the cell by hook or by crook, or with the permission of the police authorities, to ask me questions on any developments in the country and give me the news behind the headlines. I treasured the moments I shared with them, for I knew that whatever they were able to publish would keep a large number of people informed of my whereabouts and my state of mind.

But above all, I had a constant stream of Ogoni visitors. It isn't necessary to detail all those who came calling, as every day they came in batches from all parts of Ogoni and beyond, offering us solidarity, comfort – and money! If there was anything which buoyed me up, it was this show of loyalty and solidarity from the Ogoni people. From far away Lagos, the Ogoni community sent a delegation with words of comfort and 2,000 naira which I requested them to pay to MOSOP, as I did not need the money. I imagined to what length they would have gone to collect they money, and I was touched, deeply touched.

My detention had the potential of destabilising the MOSOP, more so as Dr Leton and Edward Kobani had resigned their positions. But the remaining members of the Steering Committee got together, formally elected a new executive and got down to business. I was elected President, *in absentia*, Ledum Mitee became Deputy President, Father Kabari, an Oxford University-trained Catholic priest, was elected Treasurer and Simeon Idemyor was made Financial Secretary. Dr Ben Naanen, a bright and up-coming historian of the University of Port Harcourt, remained Secretary. There were also six Vice-Presidents, all of them much younger than me, representing each of the six Ogoni kingdoms. This was definitely a much stronger team than we had had in the past, and infinitely more committed.

I also came to learn that certain people who were seen as traitors to the Ogoni cause had found it quite difficult to remain in Ogoni, and had taken refuge in Port Harcourt as guests of Governor Ada George. This group consisted largely of four of the six government-appointed chiefs in Ogoni. There were others too.

The most important of them was Edward Kobani. He too came to see me with his wife, the gentle and beautiful Rose. I saw Edward regard the cell in which we were kept with some satisfaction. And when he opened his mouth to speak, it was to remind me that I had once said that the revolution would invariably claim its victims. The implication was that I was its first victim. I did not mind that, I thought. But when he began to complain about his inability to get to his hometown, Bodo, because of fear of reprisals from the youth of the place, I knew that he needed a discussion with me.

I have known Edward Kobani since childhood. He grew up in Bori where his father was a court clerk. He was a student at he University College, Ibadan, and we often met at annual meetings of the Ogoni Students Union.

By 1961, when I began to cast about to form the Ogoni Divisional Union, Edward had graduated from the University. He became an official of one of the fringe political parties in Nigeria at the time, the Dynamic Party. I believe that Edward contested an election in Ogoni on the platform of the party and failed, although he would have been a better candidate than the winner of the election. In Eastern Nigeria at the time you would have to have been exceptionally strong to have won an election against the government party, the National Council of Nigeria and the Cameroons (NCNC).

By 1962, when I got to the University of Ibadan, Edward Kobani was teaching in another private secondary school in Port Harcourt, Niger Grammar School. In my first long vacation of June 1963, I found a job in Port Harcourt and, having nowhere to stay in the town, was offered a room in the flat which Edward was occupying with his young Ogoni bride, Rose. I also spent the 1964 long vacation as his guest, and when I graduated in 1965, before I rented a flat while I taught at Stella Maris College in Port Harcourt, I was also his guest. I was never to forget this kindness, which Edward offered me when it mattered most.

I learnt a lot in his company, meeting a great number of young graduates who were his contemporaries at the University of Ibadan and who now occupy various positions in the country. One of the people to whom Edward introduced me was the late Dr Obi Wali, who was to become a close friend and a mentor. Edward was also endowed, in the best traditions of the Ogoni, with wit, humour and *bonhomie*.

138

We discussed politics, both national and local, and worked at the Ogoni Divisional Union of which he was President and I, Secretary. He was anti-establishment, a fact which I liked at that time of my life, more so as the establishment was seen as inept and corrupt, and definitely oppressive of the Ogoni people. We often dreamt of transforming Nigerian society for the better.

When the opportunity came in 1966 for us to initiate that transformation, Edward and I were at the meetings of the Rivers Leaders of Thought at Port Harcourt, where we took the decision to ask for the creation of Rivers State by decree. For reasons of my health, I was absent at the signature session and Edward signed on behalf of the Ogoni. This was right, anyway, since he was much better known than I was.

When war broke out in 1967 and I decided to cross the fighting lines to identify with the Federal government, Edward was one of the few whom I took into confidence.

At the end of the civil war, I was on hand to get Edward and his family out of the refugee camp at Etche, and I regarded it as my responsibility to ensure that he was properly rehabilitated. I introduced him to the new administration of which I was a part, and before long Edward had become a Commissioner and member of the Executive Council of Rivers State.

For doing this, I was to receive a lot of flak from his erstwhile Ogoni colleagues in the Biafran venture, including most prominently, Dr Leton. They never tired of telling me what a dishonourable fellow Edward was, and they considered that my putting him on a pedestal was a fatal flaw in my make-up. I didn't believe them.

However, I was soon to get evidence that the Ogoni élite who had returned from Biafra resented me. I put it all down to the gerontocratic nature of Ogoni society which decrees that age is synonymous with wisdom and that no son should be greater than his father. For the Ogoni who were older than me, my 'rise' wasn't acceptable. I should have learnt to take my place in the queue behind them.

Being in government was no big deal, as far as I was concerned, and being away from it would only free me to do all those things which I really wanted to do but couldn't find the time for.

In the meantime, I had a lot to be dissatisfied with in the administration: the inefficiency, the dictatorial nature of decision-making, the corruption, the tribalism which again placed the Ogoni people at a clear disadvantage, I wanted to resign my job. Pressure was brought upon me not to do so by a large number of Ogoni people whose interest and protection my presence in government served. And so I remained as an historian of the system. But it couldn't be sustained. I became more strident in my criticisms and was appropriately given the boot unceremoniously in March 1973.

By then I had come the conclusion that there was need to split Rivers State, as the interests of the ten-odd ethnic groups in it could not be meaningfully reconciled. Along with my colleagues in the cabinet, notably Dr Obi Wali and Mr Nwobidike Nwanodi, I began, in 1974, the argument for the creation of a Port Harcourt State which would include all the non-Ijaws in Rivers State who happened to live on the plains north of the Niger River Delta proper. Edward Kobani leant his full weight to the argument.

When the state government was dismissed following the military coup of 1975, all of us became private citizens, but we continued to put our argument. By 1977, arrangements were being made for a constituent assembly and I decided to contest a seat in it. To cut a long story short, Edward Kobani led the effort to ensure that I didn't get there. Dirty tricks eventually won the day and even when I went on appeal, the judge told me his hands were tied and he could not but dismiss the appeal.

Shortly thereafter, I met in Lagos a notable journalist, Uche Chukwumerije, who was playing a prominent role in the Babangida maladministration. He had been a contemporary of Edward's at University College, Ibadan. As I rode with him in his car, he told me stories of Edward at Ibadan: how he had planned with other students on a fence-breaking riot but chickened out on D-day; how he had secured for himself a trip to Switzerland offered by Amorc, the private society, at the expense of another student; and so on and so forth

Thereafter, I didn't have to be told that I needed to give Ogoni politics a wide berth. Which I did. Having decided that I wouldn't involve myself in politics local or national, until I had developed myself properly, this didn't prove difficult at all.

What returned me to Ogoni politics again was the quest for Ogoni identity and the survival of the Ogoni people. There was need to take everybody on board, and particularly the spoilers among the Ogoni. I also knew that whatever the case, Edward would always stand for the interest of the Ogoni people. But would he be able to sustain it? That was the question.

As he sat before me in long robes that dismal afternoon, complaining that Ogoni youths would not allow him into his hometown, Bodo, I began to get angry. There was I, unable to take a walk outside of my detention cell without an armed guard following me, in a place 150 kilometres from my hometown, and unsure what the next day would bring, with a draconian law prescribing death hanging around my neck, being asked to feel pity for a man who was free to do everything else but face the anger of young men whose future they thought he had mortgaged. I gave him the length of my tongue. I reminded him how he and others had conspired to issue an announcement in my name. He denied having been a part of the plot. I assured him that it was that action which loused up all the arrangements I had made to ensure that the elections went on smoothly, with all those who wanted to vote being allowed to do so. There were some more arguments.

Edward and I often disagreed, but we always got together again. I was close to some of his children and to his wife, Rose.

Indeed, one of his children, Tombari, had designed the MOSOP flag. Edward's visit worsened my ill health, which was my main worry at the time. He was plain bad news that day.

In detention, the restriction of movement didn't bother me much. I was quite used to a sedentary life, and even when free would sit at my desk in my office from nine in the morning till ten at night. And back at home, after dinner, I would go into my study after a brief rest and work until two in the morning before I would have my usual four-hour sleep.

At Owerri, Dube and Nwiee and I would wake up at six o'clock to perform our ablutions. I would get dressed, go downstairs into the courtyard, take a walk the length of the open courtyard several times, counting number of paces, and then return to the cell, have a breakfast of fruit and whatever, then wait to receive visitors. By evening, when the visitors would have thinned out, I would again do a turn in the yard before returning to the cell to prepare for a long night, reading, listening to the radio, and chanting with Dube.

I had known Dube for quite a while. He had come to me years back, having just completed his studies in printing at Manchester University. He needed office space to carry on his private business, but had no money. I offered him one of the spare rooms below my office and he set up in business there. He often came to talk to me and I found him engaging and energetic. Watching his seriousness of purpose, I often did regret what few openings there were for him, merely because he was Ogoni. In Hausaland, he would have held the exalted post of government printer. But here he was, scrounging around for a living. When we started MOSOP, he threw his boundless energy into it and became virtually indispensable to the Steering Committee.

Kabari Nwiee, the other detainee, I had never seen in all my life until that night when we fetched him from the police cell in Abagana. It transpired that he was a father of nine children from two wives. He had been chairman of NYCOP in his village of Opuoko. My childhood friend, Mr Lah-Loolo, had taken exception to something he did or did not do and had reported him to the police, which was how he ended up in illegal detention. Just that. He was a small fry, given to few words, or so I thought, until, one day, he had a drop of alcohol, or what Nigerians call 'hot drink', and then the words came tumbling out of him like water from a spigot.

My discussions with Dube invariably centred around the Ogoni and their problems. We analysed and thought about the struggles of MOSOP, the future of the struggle and what else we might expect. And it was comforting that there was someone to share these thoughts with.

In such times, poetry comes handy. And I did write poems for my late son, Tedum, which I somehow lost, and the single anthem for Ogoni which appeared first in my Khana mother-tongue:

> *Yoor Zaansin Ogoni*
> Bari a dem Ogoni
> Le buen ka le zor
> Fo efeloo le wereloo
> Doo kor zian aa I le yee
> Ne i o suanu le ekpo
> E ema ba pya baa
> Bari a dem Ogoni
> Le buen ka le zor
> Ne I o leelee denden son
> Kwa dee ne pya Gokana
> Khana, Eleme, Tai le Babbe
> Doo lo Ogoni lu ka

> Which, translated into English, reads:
> Creator of Ogoni
> Land of glory and wealth
> Grant us thy peace and lasting love
> Plant justice over our land
> Give us thy wisdom and the strength

To shame our enemies
Creator of Ogoni
Land of glory and wealth
Grant everlasting blessings Lord
To people of Gokana
Khana, Eleme, Tai and Babbe
Glorious Ogoni land

And so the days passed. We were now waiting for the hearing of the action we had instituted, which was fixed for 10 July.

Before that event, Claude Ake came calling. His visit was very important to me, psychologically. It was the first time a prominent non-Ogoni person visited us. I had noted that so far, not one person from other parts of Rivers State, including those with whom I had worked in the Rivers State Study Group where we examined the problems which assailed the peoples of the state, had come to visit with us in solidarity.

Claude was entirely of a different breed. A political scientist, he was educated at Kings College, Lagos, the University of Ibadan and Columbia University, where he taught before proceeding to the Chair of Political Economy at universities in Canada, Dar es Salaam and Nairobi. In 1977, he took up the Chair of Political Economy at the University of Port Harcourt and became Dean of the Faculty of the Social Sciences there. Highly respected in academic circles world-wide, he had won the Nigerian National Merit Award in 1992, in addition to being the only black man in the American Social Science Academy. He was later made a member of the New York Academy of Science.

I had only started to associate with him in 1989. I met him in Washington, DC 1990 when I was touring as a Distinguished Visiting Fellow of the United States Information Agency. He was then at the Brookings Institution. He had set up the Centre for Advanced Social Studies, an independent think-tank, in 1991 in Port Harcourt, and was clearly a very valuable man to have around.

He had been abroad at the time of my arrest, and only came to know about it when he read Tony Daniel's piece on it in *The Times Literary Supplement*. He returned to Nigeria and, the very next day, spent five hours with us at Owerri. In that time, we analysed, discussed, X-rayed and thought of my situation. He did everything to comfort me, and showed intense concern for Dube and Nwiee, feeling happy that I was sharing a cell with them. It was from him I gathered that interest in my arrest had been aroused in Britain, in particular, but also elsewhere. When he eventually left in mid-afternoon, I felt relieved, grateful, joyful and even fulfilled.

I had been impressing on the Owerri police the need to let me have proper medical attention. Dr Idoko was around on a daily basis to check my blood pressure and to do whatever he could to reassure me. He had recommended that I be transferred to a clinic, but the decision rested with his supervisors and they were taking their time over it. They probably had to refer the case to Lagos for a decision. Which meant that if I had to die, Lagos would determine it. They were surely playing!

A bit of drama was not lacking either. On the Thursday afternoon, a man with a briefcase came barging into the cell. He looked scruffy and ungainly.

'Do you need any help?' he asked.

'What sort of help?' I demanded.

'Bail. Or something like that.'

'Our lawyer is arranging for bail.'

'Then you will never leave here.'

'Why not?'

'Lawyers are no use. They only complicate things for people in police custody. They complicate things.' He shook his head in commiseration with people who are in police custody and seek the assistance of lawyers.

'I don't understand,' I said.

'You see, today is Thursday. Tomorrow is Friday. On Fridays, the senior officers who give approval are in meetings the whole day. There is no-one to sign the bail. Lawyers

145

cannot get into the meeting. They are too big. Besides, they have to go to court. I can wait all day for the senior officers to finish their meeting and have the papers signed. And, you know, if you don't get bailed on Friday, you have to stay in the cell until Monday. That's not good.'

I thanked the 'bail expert' for the information, and he left, a trifle disappointed. And I was left to ponder what men often do to earn a living!

Chapter Nine

THE approval for me to move to the police clinic had come that Thursday, 8 July. I expected to be produced in court the next day, but that did not materialise because the summons had not been served on the police – or so they claimed. The judge ordered that we be produced on 13 July.

The 'O/C Admin' was a very important man in police headquarters, and you felt it at every point. The incumbent was a tall, black man with a developing paunch. If I had to move to the clinic, only he could sanction it and make arrangements for me to move. All day Thursday he found it impossible to conclude arrangements for a vehicle that would drive me to my new abode, which was no more than a mile away. Not all the pressure in the world would move him from his accustomed speed of action. There were just too many obstacles in the way. The papers he had to sign, the orders he had to give, the myriad things he had to supervise. The 'O/C Admin' was a man of power in an inefficient place.

When everything official failed, he had to do me a favour, the next day. He took me in his personal car to the clinic. I sat between two armed police guards for the 10-minute drive through dirt roads, farm patches and ill-constructed, ugly houses. Dr Idoko was not immediately available to receive me upon arrival, but soon showed up and made me welcome. The clinic itself was a new one, and I was the first patient to use it. That is not to say that it was spick and span and everything in place or in good working order. Far from it. It had been constructed in the usual slap-dash manner of Nigerian official contract jobs, no doubt at ten times the usual cost, and opened with a fanfare by the wife of no less a personality than the Inspector-General of Police, after whom (the wife, I mean) it was appropriately named.

It was only after I had been officially admitted that curtains of some sort were crudely hung on the front windows whose louvered shutters would not open. I had to buy a bedsheet for a long window which gave out on to a corridor separating the ward from the bathroom and toilet.

The ward itself had four beds on which no-one had slept so far. All in all, it was much better than my previous cell. There was absolute quiet all around, the building being far apart from other buildings in the area and separated from them, as it was, by farm patches. I had my first bath in two weeks! While in the cell at the police headquarters, I had contented myself with towelling myself down each morning and night.

Before leaving for the clinic, I had worried myself to no end as what would happen to Dube and Nwiee. I had pleaded with Assistant Commissioner of Police Ilozuoke to leave them in the room we had been using and desist from sending them into the guardroom. He was not forthcoming in this regard. It continued to be a point of anxiety. Separated from both of them, I was concerned about their welfare. I had left them with some money for their food, although Dube's staff and family often made the long journey from Port Harcourt to bring him food, which he shared with Nwiee, whom no-one came to see.

On hand to guard me at the clinic were six armed men of the Police Mobile Force, who were there 24 hours a day. Each watch lasted 12 hours, sometimes 24. I noticed that they were not fed throughout, and often had to find them funds to assist with their meals.

It was not funny, this detention, in which I had to feed myself, buy my own medicine, feed my guards, and hope for the best. I often wondered how easy it would be for one of the guards to move into my room, shoot me through the head, and that would be that. I was quite sure that they would let it be known to the world that I was trying to escape when I was gunned down.

Mercifully, nothing of that sort happened. The guards proved quite friendly. Each change of duty was reported to me, and their leader would introduce himself politely. Most were familiar with my struggle, had heard of me, and were quite sympathetic. They were only doing their duty, I had to understand.

The days were full, as usual. Delegations upon delegations of Ogoni people came calling each day, and we had a lot to discuss. Always my advice was 'Get organised in your villages and your various kingdoms, along the lines established by MOSOP. Your strength lies in organisation. Avoid violence!'

We were still at the seminal level of organisation, but we had done quite well, the Ogoni people being quick on the uptake. And most were imbued with a sense of urgency, having realised that we were facing the possibility of extinction.

I believed that if we had the opportunity, we would be able, relying upon ourselves and our genius, to re-create Ogoni society. Enthusiasm was very high, most had given their time and money freely, and hopes were equally high. What I did not count on was that all this would raise the profile of the Ogoni and engineer the envy of others, so that instead of its being a model, it would be seen as something to be crushed. Even at that, I felt that the Ogoni people were being forced into a struggle, and that the process would strengthen them eventually. The price might well be worth it.

In the end, the real difficulty was having to cope with the debilitating poverty of the people. It stymied organisation, and stopped people from doing what they would like to. Casting my mind back on the mobilisation efforts which had succeeded to any extent in Nigeria, I noticed that they were all carried out against a backdrop of the possession of some

149

measure of power, and under the nose of a colonial government which was not murderous, but was guided by the rule of law. In any case, the people being mobilised were numerous enough. The Hausa-Falani, the Igbo and the Yoruba were amongst the biggest nations on earth, and although the Tiv, the other group mobilised by their leaders, were not so numerous, they were still the fifth largest ethnic group in the country, and therefore had more resources upon which to call.

All the same, the sacrifice of the youth and women of Ogoni was most encouraging. Everyone had volunteered their services and time, freely and without complaint. They took whatever tribulation that came stoically, finding instances in the Bible of similar events. Mostly, they relied on the journey of the Israelites from Egypt to the Promised Land, and in many cases, I received homilies on the life of Moses, who, they insisted, was my model.

Apart from the Ogoni people, I also had a few other visitors, particularly the writer Charry Ada Onwu, an energetic and powerful lady if ever there was one, who came in the company of another member of the Imo branch of the Association of Nigerian Authors, to offer me humorous and entertaining stories.

But it was not to last. The next Monday, barely three days after I had arrived at the clinic, Olu Onagoruwa, my lawyer, came in from Lagos to appear in court the following day. He and a junior from his chambers chatted me up for about an hour or so, and then went to their hotel.

'I'll see you in court tomorrow,' he said.

'That's if the police agree to produce me.'

'They will this time. They've run out of excuses. You'll have to be granted bail.'

Cheering news, no doubt. But no sooner had he left than the Coffin arrived, bearing Mr Inah at his most lugubrious. He must have felt bad that I was in a clinic. I think he would have preferred my being in the dank, over-populated guardroom at the police headquarters or in the mortuary.

After he had exchanged a few words of greeting, he took yet another statement from me. The import of this did not strike me immediately. It was only after they had left, and another police officer came to ask after them, that I knew something was brewing.

The police officer had always been polite and extremely helpful. But that afternoon, he was not smiling. He appeared anxious. He wanted to know if Mr Inah had come to see me. I confirmed that he had.

'Where is he now?'

'I don't know. I think I overheard him say he would be leaving for Port Harcourt.'

'Port Harcourt?' There was consternation in his voice.

'Yes,' I answered. 'Is there a problem?'

'No. No. It's OK.'

'Are you coming to take me to the court tomorrow? The judge ordered you to produce me.'

'That's not in my hands. Stay well. Goodbye.'

And he left, taking long urgent strides. I watched from the window as he drove off.

I slept well that night, giving no thought to the oppressive ways of the Babangida regime. I may have taken false comfort in the reassuring presence of Olu Onagoruwa or the court order. And it was just as well that I had some relaxed sleep.

At five o'clock the next morning, the sound of the Coffin driving into the compound woke me up from sleep. The sound of the mobile police guard saluting smartly indicated that a superior officer was around. The sound of boots on the staircase. The harsh knock on the door of the ward. Mr Inah's familiar outline in the long kaftan. Behind him, another man in flowing robes who always accompanied him, but often remained in the Coffin.

'Get ready, sir, you are due to travel.'

'Where to?'

'I don't know.'

'But I'm not well.'

151

'I have my orders.'

'I'm not well enough to travel.'

'We have to go. Time is not on our side. Get ready, sir.'

'I have to see the police doctor.'

'You're only wasting time. You've always co-operated with us. Please co-operate.'

'I can't leave the clinic without the permission of the doctor.'

'You don't need his permission.'

'I do. I'm his patient. He has to confirm to me that I'm in a position to undertake a road journey in a coffin.'

'Coffin? Which coffin?'

'Your J5 bus.' I couldn't see his face in the darkness.

'We have to leave immediately. I don't want to use force.'

'Get the doctor to certify that I can leave this clinic.'

Mr Inah turned on his heels and left. While he was gone, my car, which always waited on me, turned up. The chauffeur slept in town in a friend's house. He had turned up earlier than usual. One of the guards came up to tell me that he had information that I was being taken to Port Harcourt to appear in court on a criminal charge. 'Don't agree to go with them, sir.'

I sent my chauffeur to inform Olu Onagoruwa of the latest development. He was no sooner gone than Dr Idoko turned up with Mr Inah. He went through the motion of checking my blood pressure. He said there was nothing he could do to stop the police officer from taking me away. I thanked him for his trouble and bade him goodbye.

I asked Mr Inah to allow me to bathe and get dressed. He agreed. I went through my morning ablutions deliberately, hoping that I would get word back from Olu Onagoruwa. No dice.

Before long I had dressed, packed my personal items and left them aside to be conveyed by my chauffeur back to Port Harcourt. I walked downstairs, bade the guards goodbye, and climbed into the front seat of the Coffin. Mr Inah got in after me and we drove out of the compound. There were six or so armed policemen in the back of the Coffin.

As we drove out, it struck me that in the four days I had stayed there, I had not once stepped out of doors. I had only gone downstairs once, and that was to see off Baridon and Rose Konya, possibly the most outstanding and exemplary Ogoni couple of our time, who had spent a good part of the Sunday with me.

The Coffin threaded its way back to the police headquarters and came to a stop in front of the building which I had left four days earlier. There, Dube and Nwiee joined us and we headed out of Owerri town.

The morning was bright and the air which rushed into the Coffin was refreshing. As we drove past the Concorde Hotel, where Olu Onagoruwa was lodged, I wondered if he had got my message at all. Anyway, it didn't matter anymore.

We drove the distance to Port Harcourt, stopping only once when one of the policemen wished to answer the call of nature and was allowed to do so in a nearby bush. As we got to the Port Harcourt International Airport, Mr Inah began to wonder where his boss might be. The latter was supposed to arrive by air, and Mr Inah had a mind for the Coffin to get to the airport to see if he had done so. So to the airport we went. Mr Ogbeifun was not to be found. We headed towards Port Harcourt.

I did wonder for a while where we were going. I found out soon enough as we drove into the high court premises in the centre of the town. Ready to receive us was a unit of the Police Mobile Force in glittering riot gear which seemed to have been purchased that very morning. They surrounded the magistrates' court, to which we were driven and offloaded.

I thought wistfully of the comic aspect of the event. As we drove from Owerri, we passed several cars and buses carrying hundreds of Ogoni people to the high court in Owerri, where I was to be produced by order of the judge. Ogoni men, women and youths had been there in their hundreds the previous week, and had gone home frustrated because the case had been adjourned. But that hadn't stopped them from making the long journey once again. However, whereas they were in Owerri, here were we in Port Harcourt where no-one, not even my lawyer, Ledum Mitee, knew that we would be. And in all that calm, there was a riot squad waiting for a riot they knew would not be.

We sat in court and waited while the magistrate, whom I knew to be a Mrs D, famous as a government hang-woman, if such a term exists, cleared her desk, so to speak. Within five minutes, she had adjourned the case that was before her, and then she called our case.

We stepped into the box. I was quite familiar with the court and the procedure. I waited with bated breath for the charge to be read. I could have laughed my scorn to the roof of the grimy court hall, if that would not have been regarded as being disrespectful to the court. I heard it said that we had assembled at an Ogoni village which I had not visited in all my life, there to plan I know not what. That we had designed a flag and written an anthem, and I planned I know not what against the government of Nigeria. All this amounted to a six-count charge of sedition and unlawful assembly. Did we agree to be tried in that particular court? The answer was merely perfunctory. The magistrate wrote in her book. We were guilty or not guilty? There was no reason to answer. The magistrate, Mrs D, wrote in her book.

Then she wrote in her book, and wrote in her book, the skinny young woman behind a pair of glasses. And she lifted up her face after she had written in her book, and decided that we had a case to answer. How she came to that marvellous conclusion, I don't know. She was committing us to prison custody. That was the long and short of it. It wasn't that simple, though. We had no counsel, but there were lawyers in court, all of whom were appearing for us, on a sympathy basis, I presume. The lawyer who demanded bail for us, since the offence was bailable, later came to the prison to see me. He was a Mr Briggs, who had taught at Birabi Memorial Grammar School in Bori, my home town.

Well, Mrs D was not disposed to grant us bail since, in the

opinion of the prosecuting sergeant, we would be raising hell and disturbing the peace of a whole lot of well-fed people. So to prison custody we would have to go. And, by the way, Mrs D would be going on leave shortly after turning her fine legal mind to our case. And after that, the courts would be on their annual recess, and then... and then, well, she would be disposed to hear the case again on 21 September. By which time, I quickly calculated, I would have been held for three months, which was close to the prison term of six months laid down for the offence of sedition.

I had been dragged out of a police clinic, which was less than the hospital bed I needed. Was there a chance Her Worship (Worship!) would give an order that I be sent to hospital? That was not her business, her sole business being to send us to prison custody. As Her Worship pleased.

No, I was not upset with Mrs D. I felt sorry for her, and for Mr Ogbeifun and for Mr Inah, and all those men and women who were being forced by the system to subvert the law, tell lies, play dirty tricks, in order to earn their monthly pay. I also felt terrible when I thought that the three players I have mentioned above were from ethnic minority areas, and were acting for the Hausa bandit, if Hausa he is, called Babangida, who should have been before a firing squad for treason against his country. But that momentary feeling only evoked in me a determination to pour all my resources, intellectual and otherwise, into creating a society where such things would not be. It brought forth the beginnings of a song I completed in prison a week later:

> *The True Prison*
> It is not the leaking roof
> Nor the singing mosquitoes
> In the damp, wretched cell.
> It is not the clank of the key
> As the warder locks you in.
> It is not the measly rations

Unfit for man or beast
Nor yet the emptiness of day
Dipping into the blankness of night
It is not
It is not
It is not.
It is the lies that have been drummed
Into your ears for one generation
It is the security agent running amok
Executing callous calamitous orders
In exchange for a wretched meal a day
The magistrate writing in her book
Punishment she knows is undeserved
The moral decrepitude
Mental ineptitude
Lending dictatorship spurious legitimacy
Cowardice masked as obedience
Lurking in our denigrated souls
It is fear damping trousers
We dare not wash off our urine
It is this
It is this
It is this
Dear friend, turns our free world
Into a dreary prison.

Yes, we, the MOSOP Three, were headed for Port Harcourt Prison. The police had prepared everything. As we stepped out of the magistrates' court into the Coffin, a siren wailed a shrill cry of terror, injustice and temporary triumph. A truckload of armed police followed the car blowing the siren, another Peugeot pick-up van followed the Coffin, and in another five minutes we were before the gate of Port Harcourt Prison. We got down from the Coffin, and the gate opened and let us in.

The night of 13 June, as the presidential election results were being announced, I had gone to see Lateef Jakande, sometime

Governor of Lagos State. My passport had just been seized by security agencies. And he said to startled ears, 'As the prison doors open to let you in, so will they open to let you out.'

As I stepped into Port Harcourt Prison, aka Alabama City, I recalled Jakande's words gladly.

Chapter Ten

PORT Harcourt Prison lies but a stone's throw from my 42 Aggrey Road office, and was there before I began to know Port Harcourt in 1954. It is also a stone's throw from Stella Maris College, where I had taught after graduating from university in 1965. I had never visited it. It was there, at the back of Port Harcourt, close to the marshy swamps, solid, grey, forbidding from the outside. It was always a place to be avoided.

I cast my mind back now, and think that in Ogoni society prisons did not exist. Wrongdoers were killed, fined, sent into exile or made to swear an oath. Thus, when the colonialists introduced the idea of a prison, a place of correction where wrongdoers spent time, it was novel, and has not sat well with our psyche. A prison was always a place to be avoided. Murderers and thieves were there together. No-one had reason to be there. If you were there, you had to be an outcast.

Since our denigration as a people was unprotested, no-one had ever been held on his conscience. So the fact that an innocent man could be sent to prison was unthinkable.

It is true that we had read of the detention of people in Nigeria, but it was mostly a phenomenon of Lagos, where there were several human rights activists. That was until I told the Ogoni people that they were being cheated, denied of their rights to a healthy environment, and the resources of their land. Then almost the entire 51,000 Ogoni men, women and children became activists. Still, prison seemed far away. We could understand death at the hands of a murderous army or police, but I do not think that we could understand imprisonment. And yet, I do remember that I kept warning the Ogoni people to prepare for harassment, imprisonment and death.

Altogether, it was fitting that I was one of the first to be detained. It would show subsequent detainees that they were in good company.

There were all sorts of preliminaries to be endured before one became an inmate of the prison, such as handing over all cash and other belongings to the prison authorities and being inducted into the life of the prison community.

I suppose that I was arrested as a Very Important Prisoner and therefore my story will not be as lurid as it should be. All the same, I did find the prison a very depressing place. If its exterior is solid, grey and forbidding, as I have said, its interior is grimy, squalid and dilapidated.

I must say that I find it very distasteful writing about Port Harcourt Prison. Given the way public buildings are kept throughout Nigeria, no-one will be surprised to hear that the prison was in total disrepair and unfit for human habitation.

You can tell the state of a nation by the way it keeps its prisons, prisoners being mostly out of sight. On this criterion, Nigeria was in a parlous state indeed.

The prison had been built in colonial times; it was, at that time, the largest prison in West Africa, and was well laid out, with plenty of open space for fresh air, and all educational facilities, such as workshops and a library. It also had an infirmary. It had, and still has, a women's wing. But everything was in disrepair, everything was collapsing, everything was gone.

The administrative block itself had not been painted for ages; the room where the senior prison officers worked was stuffy and dirty, furnished with old chairs and tables, without fans or air-conditioners. There was no telephone, only one water closet which was kept strictly for the boss of the prison, and no one there had a car. Oh, the wretchedness of it all was scandalous. And there are Nigerians who have been Ministers of Internal Affairs and supervised all this, and not said a word? More, there are prominent Nigerians who have been held under these conditions and have come out and done nothing about it.

I hadn't been in the prison for more than a day when I knew the condition of Nigerian prisons and prisoners would be added to the long list of campaigns I had already accumulated.

After we had gone through the motions of being properly registered, our property logged, our weight and height recorded, and so on and so forth, we were invited upstairs to meet the boss of the establishment, a Mr Ikpatti. This was a special treatment, because, as I have said, I was a special. Mr Ikpatti, a short man with a developing paunch, well spoken and rather kindly looking, introduced me to the ways of 'Alabama City', the nickname of the place. How it got the name, I don't know, but from what I heard officially, I knew that I was in a different world indeed.

Theoretically, everything was being done to ensure that prisoners or those in prison custody had as proper a life as the deprivation of their liberty would allow. In practice, what we had in Port Harcourt Prison was a travesty. And that probably wasn't because the government had failed to put money into it. The negligence, callousness and incompetence of some thieving officials who had run the place over the years had a lot to do with it. To cut a long story short, Mr Ikpatti welcomed me to 'Alabama City' and hoped that I would have a good time there.

I thanked him and, based on what he had told me, applied for and got permission to feed myself. I knew that Nigerian prison food was not edible; in any case, I need a special diet for survival, and only my family can provide that in Nigeria. And I obtained special permission to stay in the infirmary, since I needed medical care.

I got to the infirmary late that afternoon, the admission formalities having last four or five hours. One look at the infirmary, and my heart fell. It was leaking like a sieve; there was no ceiling; the entire place was damp; there was only a bucket latrine; the narrow beds had rotten mattresses; and heavens, what else was there not, in that place?

It didn't come as a surprise. I asked that my office send three mattresses to us, along with bedding and a lot of cleansing material – detergents, disinfectants, insecticide, anything to help us clean the wretched place.

I hadn't eaten all day, and when dinner finally came from my house at about 6.30 pm, I found I had no appetite for it. It had to be tasted first by whoever brought it – in this case, my steward – and I had to eat it in the presence of the warders, in a dingy front cubicle. No, I needed to get into the rhythm of the prison. In my state of mind I could take anything for the cause I believed in, but I did need a certain acclimatisation at every new turn of events.

Already a crowd of Ogoni people had begun to gather before the prison gates. One of the earliest callers was Mrs Z, a lawyer and daughter of Mr Nunieh, the first Ogoni lawyer, who, I was later to learn, had gone to Owerri to represent me alongside Olu Onagoruwa, Ledum Mitee and Samuel Ibgara (a childhood friend, and younger son of one of the landlords of Bori). About 800 Ogoni people had, indeed, gone to Owerri, only to learn that I had been sent to Port Harcourt. A number of them now attempted to see me in the latter place. In the end, I reluctantly had to place a limit on the number of people I would see. I didn't do this in order to keep away from visitors. But each time a visitor came, I would have to be sent for from my cell, some distance away. And I really couldn't cope with the continual coming and going.

I finally got my mattress and the other items I had ordered from my office at about nine o'clock, and went to bed there after. Next to me in the infirmary was a young Ogoni boy who had spent three years or more in the prison, waiting for someone to sign a bail of 5,000 Naira* on his behalf.

*130 Naira is approximately US$1

Apart from Dube and Nwiee, who naturally stayed with me, there were three or four young men in the ward who introduced themselves to us. They gave us an idea of how the ward was run. We had to pay a levy of a 100 naira each, which was used for the upkeep of the ward: to replace electric bulbs, etc, etc. I knew it was illegal, but didn't bother myself with that.

I slept well that night. The only problem I had was when the warder locked us in for the night. That was a novel experience, and I hated it thoroughly. What if I needed medical attention at night? There was no telephone, and no doctor either. Mercifully, the University of Port Harcourt Teaching Hospital was, literally, around the corner. But I would need to get there! I had to call on my store of humour to internalise the experience quickly and accept it as 'one of those things'.

I woke up after my usual four-hour sleep to analyse my new situation. What came to my mind was how often a prison had featured in my fiction. There were *Prisoners of Jebs* and its sequel, *Pita Dumbrok's Prison*. And in 1992, I had completed *Lemona*, my fifth novel, in longhand – only to have it stolen, along with my briefcase at Lagos Airport. I was returning from my trip to Geneva to present the Ogoni case before the United Nations Working Group on Indigenous Populations. I thought how much better the novels might have been if I had written them after my current experience. The loss of my last novel, whose heroine had spent 25 years in prison, had affected me badly, killing my desire to write fiction. I hoped that I would be able to find the will to rewrite the novel and that it would be much enriched by my experience of prisons.

I thought, too, of the other harrowing discovery that one third of the 1,200 inmates of that prison were Ogoni people. Most of them had just been dumped there on minor charges, forgotten by the police and the judicial system which sent them there, with no-one to take up their cases and give them justice. My attention had been drawn to the fact by the fairly large number of prison staff who happened to be Ogoni. Again, that was not surprising: the conditions of service of prison staff were dismal, and the salary a mere pittance. Who would want to work in the prison except the condemned of the earth?

My enemies were soon to capitalise on the fact of the number of Ogoni people on the staff. When day broke, and the workforce had their usual morning briefing, the Ogoni staff were told that they were not to get too close to me, as information had reached the authorities that there was a plan to storm the prison and effect my release. I had to work quickly to dispel that piece of blackmail. I had a press release issued to the effect that there was no need to seek my release from detention, as every day I spent there helped to advance my cause.

All that day I had a steady stream of visitors, some of whom I couldn't refuse to see, as they had travelled a long distance from Ogoni in order to meet me. My aged parents came calling also, and it was quite cheering to see them look so brave. I had initially asked my brother Owens not to allow them to come to Owerri. I had forewarned my father two years earlier that I might well end up in prison or in the grave for my endeavours, and he certainly seemed to take it well. But Owens had informed me how badly my father really felt, and I had then thought that he should not be made to suffer any more. At 89, he did not have to take the trouble to come to far-away Owerri. But when I read a brave interview which my mother gave to a national newspaper and heard her insist that I must carry on the struggle, I had no more worries about them coming to see me in detention.

And so they did come to Owerri. My father appeared quite calm, but my mother looked shaken. I had to assure her that I was perfectly all right, and that there was nothing to worry about. Like all mothers, she was solicitous of my well-being and had brought along a delicacy which I enjoyed in my youth: nutless palm fruit. I had quite forgotten it, not having had any for 40 years or so. I was really thrilled to eat them. And after she had left, I was moved to song:

Mama came calling
She came visiting today
The Lovely little lady
In her hand a dainty meal
Of nutless palm fruits
A long-forgotten delicacy
From my childhood days
Into which I dug my teeth
As my baby gums her breasts
And found therein once again
The milky sweet of a mother's blessings

On the visit to Port Harcourt Prison, the laugh was at the expense of my father. When he came to Owerri he had not told me of the birth of his youngest son, my youngest half-brother, on the day of my arrest, 21 June. Indeed, everyone had forgotten to mention it to me; it came to me via a publication in a national newspaper. When my father came visiting, I teased him no end. The grand old man only smiled.

In the first two days in the prison, I worked very hard at adapting myself to the routine of the place. Because we were in prison custody, and also in the infirmary, we were not really subject to the full routine of prison, although we had the rights to which prisoners were entitled. One major problem was again the WC facility and especially – eventually – being forced to use the bucket latrine. Ugh! But having used it once, I learnt to endure it.

Company was not lacking in the prison. Perhaps the most celebrated man there was Major-General Lekwot, who had governed Rivers State between 1975 and 1979. He was the victim of one of the worst cases of political injustice – the notorious Zangon Kataf affair, in which a minority ethnic group, the Katafs, had risen against their Hausa-Fulani oppressors. The latter had taken heavy reprisals: a phoney tribunal had been set up, before which a group of hapless Katafs, most of whom had nothing to do with the actual uprising, were arraigned and condemned to death. Babangida had granted them a reprieve, changing their sentences to various prison terms. The affair had aroused national and international furore; but injustice prevailed, and Lekwot and his kinsmen remained in jail.

I found them all, and Lekwot in particular, in a calm frame of mind. He did his exercises regularly, and I had to pass by his cell, a sort of VIP abode, each morning as I went to have my bath in a stone enclosure in the open air. We got talking, and analysed the national, Kataf and Ogoni situations.

Also in prison was Mr O C Nsirim, who was having to clear his name over the murder of my dear friend, the late Dr Obi Wali. I had a lot of difficulty talking with him, not unnaturally. I had known him for a long time, and when he slumped on the Thursday or Friday morning in his cell, there was cause for concern. I called on him once to extend my sympathy. He recovered and left the prison before I did.

The prison day was quite long, starting at about six o'clock, when the nightsoil man came to clear the latrine bucket. Some of the longer-serving inmates engaged him in a humorous banter in Igbo. Then would follow the general cleaning, and after that breakfast. I took a look once at the food that was being served and almost puked. It was fit neither for man nor beast. Thereafter, for me, it was a matter of receiving visitors, having read the newspapers which arrived with my breakfast. There was a bit of time to read, and I followed the news on my radio very keenly. The day ended at about seven o'clock when the warders locked us in. Quite dreary, I would think, and not meant to keep one in good health.

By Friday my health had deteriorated. I still hadn't had the opportunity to see my doctor, even though I requested it the very day I got to the prison. Instead of my doctor, the Coffin turned up, bearing in its depths Mr Ogbeifun and his man Friday. We went through the process of my making another written statement and answering a few more silly questions from Mr Inah. I specifically asked Mr Obgeifun if he meant to

165

transfer me again to another prison. He lied to me and swore that that was not the case.

That evening, it became imperative for me to consult a doctor. I sent for my brother Owens, who happened to be around, and asked him to get in touch by all means with Dr Ibiama, who had been looking after me. Bobo Ibiama, a consultant physician, had been my contemporary at Ibadan University. He had spent all his working life in Rivers State, where he rose to become Director of Medical Services before retiring into private practice and consulting for the University of Port Harcourt Teaching Hospital. He had lately made an unexpected foray into politics, contesting the position of the Governor of Rivers State. He was too fine a man to win a Nigerian election and duly crashed out. Very well born to a bonny family, he was a model gentleman, and came into the prison as soon as he heard of my condition.

Along with him came Professor Claude Ake, all anxious for me. Bobo took a look at me, applied his stethoscope and sphygmomanometer and decided that I had to be moved to the teaching hospital. He gave orders to that effect.

Effecting the order was to take all of the time and patience of Professor Ake, my brother Owens, my friend, Alfred Ilenre, who had come down from Lagos to see me, and one of the prison officers, Mr Okpoko, who had gone out of his way to ensure that I was properly taken care of.

It transpired that, because I was in prison custody, I remained the responsibility of the Nigerian police force and not the Nigerian prison service, and that the permission of the Rivers State Commissioner of Police would have to be obtained before I could be released into hospital. When the Commissioner of Police was contacted very late that night, he said we would require a court order from a high court judge. No judge could be contacted that night.

The following morning, Saturday, my brother was able to obtain the high court order, but when it was presented to the Commissioner of Police, a bovine-looking man called Bayo

Balogun, he merely threw the court order to the floor. This took place before a journalist of the respected newspaper *The Times* of London. And there the matter might have ended.

All that Saturday I was in agony. Then came the Sunday. I met with *The Times* reporter, Mr Kyle, and came to learn that there had been quite some concern in Britain over my safety. Indeed, Claude Ake had given me that morning a copy of *The Times Literary Supplement* in which Tony Daniels had done a piece about my arrest.

I had met Tony, an exciting medical doctor whose wanderlust has carried him through most of Africa, in March at my Port Harcourt office, and swapped stories with him. He had a wonderful fund of jokes on Africa. He had also written several travel books and I thought it really good of him to have expressed my travails to the British public.

That Sunday night when my condition deteriorated further, I had to cry for help through the window of our ward. A helpless warder came round, and sent for the Superintendent; he turned up, equally helpless, looked through my window and mumbled something really inane. I might just as well have died. But I was determined not to give my tormentors that comfort. The will to survive saw me through the crisis.

When morning came, I sent urgently to the boss of the prison and challenged him. I virtually called him an assassin before most of his senior staff whom he had invited along. I could not understand, I said, why he had refused to send me to hospital, in spite of a consultant's order. I refused to accept that the police should determine what happens to me. The prison authorities and Mr Ikpatti himself, personally, would have a lot of accounting to do to my family and to the Ogoni people if anything should happen to me because they were dithering over who was to sign what paper, or because they did not know what to do about simple matters of life and death. Somehow, it worked. After a six-hour wait, during which Mr Ikpatti must have consulted the gods and oracles of his native Ibibioland, he finally informed me that he had found a way round he regulations. He would send me to the hospital and inform the Divisional Police Officer, a minor official in the pecking order, about what he had done. It would be up to the DPO to send the information to his superiors.

Then another real problem cropped up. The prison had no writing-paper, and all the shops had closed. Mr James Nwibana, a printer from Ogoni, had visited me the previous day and left me a ream of paper, just in case I wanted to write. I sent for the paper and offered to type the letter myself just in case the prison typist had gone home.

Mercifully, the typist was an Ogoni man who had refused to close for the day. He finally typed the letter without an error, and I was on my way to the University of Port Harcourt Teaching Hospital. The prison had no ambulance and no car, of course. I had to travel in a car provided by my office, in between prison officers.

We drove past my office on Aggrey Road, and were, within a few minutes, at the blessed hospital. Mrs Beredugo, an experienced Matron and the wife of an old friend, was on duty, and took steps to ensure that I was safely installed in a private room in the hospital within a very short time indeed. Dr Ibiama had left orders to that effect. I was under sedation before long.

Believe it or not, 15 minutes after I left 'Alabama City' for the hospital, an order signed by the Chief Judge of Rivers State arrived, asking that the MOSOP Three be transferred to different prisons. I was to be sent to Enugu, and Dube and Nwiee to Owerri Prison. Mr Inah was on hand to execute the order, and only waited until midnight to commence operations.

He arrived at the prison with armed guards, ordered Dube and Nwiee to get ready, then hurled them into the Coffin, and came to the teaching hospital to fetch me. I was rudely awakened out of deep sleep to see the unwelcome face of Mr Inah at the door.

'I have orders to take you away,' Mr Inah intoned coldly.

'Where to?'

'To Enugu.'

I looked at the time. It was thirty minutes past midnight.

'Sorry, I'm not well,' I said weakly.

'I have my orders.'

The Matron on duty came to ask what was happening.

Mr Inah reported his mission.

'Sorry, you can't take away the patient without the specific instructions of the Chief Medical Director.'

'I have my orders, madam,' Mr Inah emphasised.

'And I have my orders too!' The Matron was firm.

'Mr Inah withdrew. I could hear the rain pouring down.

'Don't worry,' the Matron assured me, as she tucked me into my bed. 'Nobody will take you away from here.'

Later that night, Dr Longjohn, my contemporary at Ibadan University and a friend from those days, turned up. He woke me up and asked if I had been taken proper care of.

I replied in the affirmative.

'That's fine. You can go back to sleep.'

I rolled over. Dr Longjohn had just saved me from the conspiracy which involved Governor Ada George, the Commissioner of Police, Bayo Balogun, and other highly placed persons in the murderous Babangida regime.

Fate had played its own part. That night, Mr Ogbeifun and Bayo Balogun did their damnedest to find the leader of the police mobile squadron to organise men to storm the hospital and take me away. That man was not to be found. And they gave up reluctantly.

Dube was in the Coffin while Mr Inah drove around looking for the Chief Medical Director of the teaching hospital, the Police Mobile Force leader, the Commissioner of Police and Mr Ogbeifun. According to him, they finally drove off when all else failed, at about two o'clock, in the direction of Owerri. Arriving at the Port Harcourt International Airport, Mr Inah decided that he needed some sleep, and the Coffin stopped at the airport so he could do so. They arrived at

Owerri Prison at nine o'clock the following morning. The prison authorities were not very willing to take them in, as the regulations had been breached. In the end, they were admitted.

That morning, Dr Longjohn came to inform me, humorously, that he had been told that Ogoni warriors would be coming to the hospital. Was I assuring him that that wouldn't happen? I gave him the undertaking. He laughed and went off.

Unknown to me, a great number of people and organisations, in Nigeria and abroad, had taken steps to save me from the fangs of Babangida, the Monster of Minna. Amnesty International, which had adopted the three of us as Prisoners of Conscience, *The Times* of London, *The Observer,* the Committee of Writers in Prison of International PEN, the BBC, Ken Jr, my first son, William Boyd, the peerless British novelist, the United Nations Working Group for Indigenous People, UNPO, Greenpeace, The Association of Nigerian Authors: all had played a role in my release. Nor must I fail to mention the staff in my office at Port Harcourt and Lagos, Apollos Onwuasoaku, Innocent Iheme, Deebii Nwiado, Emeka Nwachukwu, Kweku Arthur, Sunday Dugbor and others. And of course, the entire people of Ogoni, Olu Onagoruwa, Ledum Mitee and Barry Kumbe, Senator Cyprus Ninieh, Samuel Igbara and Mr Briggs, the lawyer who took up my cause free of charge. I must also thank the senior police officers at Owerri, including Mr Ilozuoke and Mr Ukah, the prison officers at Port Harcourt Prison, Dr II Ibiama and the doctors and nurses at the University of Port Harcourt Teaching Hospital.

Release finally came on 22 July, when one of the police officers in mufti who had abducted me on the highway in June came to inform me that he had instruction to grant me bail. This instruction, it would appear, had come from someone called Aikhomu, who was said to be Vice-President of some place called Nigeria. Just where were the courts, you wonder? What of Mrs D, the magistrate who was busy writing in her book and sending us to prison custody? The court no longer mattered. A man called Aikhomu had decided. Shame on these men, who subvert the law and morality! The bail bond, I was told, could only be signed by my 89-year-old father. I'm stumped if these guys haven't all gone crazy. I thanked the messenger for his troubles, anyway.

Meanwhile, in Owerri, by the crazed dance of Nigerian masquerade, the good judge who sat over my suit, which we continued to press, had found that the state had held me illegally, and ruled that I be paid some compensation and set free. The ruling did not matter to the Babangida government: it had already taken a decision, unguided by the law which it was supposed to be obeying.

I had been detained for a month and a day, during which I had witnessed the efficiency of evil. In a country where virtually nothing worked, the security services, armed with all the gadgets of modern invention, made sure that all orders were carried out with military precision. And the men were marvellously faithful to their instructions.

Mr Ogbeifun and Mr Inah turned up at my bedside to say something about bail and whatnot, I could only offer them the scorn of stony silence, my eyes shut, so I wouldn't see their extraordinarily handsome faces.

Had I known what the conspiracy had in store for the Ogoni people, I might not have been so thankful that I had got off lightly. Notice had been given that on 15 July, 132 Ogoni men, women and children, returning from their abode in the Cameroons, had been waylaid on the Andoni River by an armed gang and cruelly murdered, leaving but two women to make a report.

The genocide of the Ogoni had taken on a new dimension. The manner of it I will narrate in my next book, if I live to tell the tale.

Port Harcourt
17 May 1994

171

PART II

Statement Ken Saro-Wiwa was prevented from reading, 10 November 1995

Ken Saro-Wiwa's closing statement
to the Military Appointed Tribunal
(Justice Ibrahim Auta)

My Lord,

We all stand before history. I am a man of peace, of ideas. Appalled by the denigrating poverty of my people who live on a richly endowed land, distressed by their political marginalization and economic strangulation, angered by the devastation of their land, their ultimate heritage, anxious to preserve their right to life and to a decent living, and determined to usher to this country as a whole a fair and just democratic system which protects everyone and every ethnic group and gives us all a valid claim to human civilization, I have devoted my intellectual and material resources, my very life, to a cause in which I have total belief and from which I cannot be blackmailed or intimidated. I have no doubt at all about the ultimate success of my cause, no matter the trial and tribulations which I and those who believe with me may encounter on our journey. No imprisonment nor death can stop our ultimate victory.

I repeat that we all stand before history. I and my colleagues are not the only ones on trial. Shell is here on trial and it is as well that it is represented by counsel said to be holding a watching brief. The company has indeed ducked this particular trial, but its day will surely come and the lessons learnt here may prove useful to it for there is no doubt in my mind that the ecological war that the company has waged in the Niger Delta will be called to question sooner than later and the crimes of that war duly punished. The crime of the company's dirty wars against the Ogoni people will also be punished.

On trial also is the Nigerian nation, its present rulers and those who assist them. Any nations which can do to the weak and disadvantaged what the Nigerian nation has done to the Ogoni people, loses a claim to independence and to freedom from outside influence. I am not one of those who shy away from protesting injustice and oppression, arguing that they are expected in a military regime. The military do not act alone. They are supported by a gaggle of politicians, lawyers, judges, academics, and businessmen, all of them hiding under the claim that they are only doing their duty, men and women too afraid to wash their pants of urine. We all stand on trial, my lord, for by our actions we have denigrated our country and jeopardised the future of our children. As we subscribe to the sub-normal and accept double standards, as we lie and cheat openly, as we protect injustice and oppression, we empty our classrooms, denigrate our hospitals, fill our stomachs with hunger and elect to make ourselves the slaves of those who ascribe to higher standards, pursue the truth, and honour justice, freedom, and hard work. I predict that the scene here will be played and replayed by generations yet unborn.

Some have already cast themselves in the role of villains, some are tragic victims, some still have a chance to redeem themselves. The choice is for each individual. I predict that the denouement of the riddle of the Niger Delta will soon come. The agenda is being set at this trial. Whether the peaceful way I have favoured will prevail depends on what the oppressor decides, what signals are sent out to the waiting public.

In my innocence of the false charges I face, in my utter conviction, I call upon the Ogoni people, the peoples of the Niger Delta, and the oppressed ethnic minorities of Nigeria to stand up now and fight fearlessly and peacefully for their rights. History is on their side. God is on their side. For the Holy Quran says in Sura 42, verse 41: 'All those that fight when oppressed incur no guilt, but Allah shall punish the oppressor.' Come the day.

Ken Saro-Wiwa's final words before he was hanged: 'Lord take my soul, but the struggle continues'.

PART III

Letters: from Ken Saro-Wiwa in prison,
and after...

All the letters to Ken Saro-Wiwa were confiscated. These are some of the letters that he wrote to family, friends and supporters during his final term in Port Harcourt Prison, Nigeria.

Who's who:
Jeje: *the name for Ken Saro-Wiwa within the family*
Junior: *Ken Wiwa, his eldest son*
Gian: *his second son*
Zina: *his daughter*
Eagle: *his brother, Owens.*
Comfort: *his younger sister.*
Majella McCarron: *a Catholic nun from Ireland who became Ken's confidante before and during his detention*
Nene: *Ken Saro-Wiwa's wife, Maria/Marian*
Olivia: *Ken Wiwa's wife*

* * *

17.9.95

Junior,
  I am beginning a hunger strike on Monday 18th September, 1995 to protest the following:

1. The declaration on August 10, 1995 of Professor Yadudu, Special Advisor on Legal Affairs to General Sani Abacha, made to the UN Committee for the Eradication of Racial Discrimination that I am guilty of murder.
2. The continued sitting of the Special Military Tribunal in spite of the governments' presumption of my guilt. The Tribunal is a charade meant to put a legal face to my predetermined conviction on false charges in a situation where I have no right of appeal.
3. The occupation by the Security Forces of my 24 Aggrey Road, Port Harcourt office from July 29, 1995 to date.
4. The raid by the Security Forces of my Lagos office on 15th September, 1995 and the seizure of my documents.
5. Dehumanizing treatment and mental torture in the military

176

camp detention centre where I am being held. I have since July 29th, 1995 been denied all reading material and access to my family.

6. The continued harassment of the Ogoni people including arbitrary arrest and detention without charges by the Rivers State Internal Security Task Force.

Please inform the BBC World Service, BBC African Service, the Voice of America and the world press of this and keep it in the public eye as long as is possible. I am being persecuted for my beliefs.

Courier mail follows to OF
Ken Saro-Wiwa

* * *

Mandy Garner
International PEN
London, UK

A year is gone since I was rudely roused from my bed and clamped into detention. Sixty-five days in chains, many weeks of starvation, months of mental torture and, recently, the rides in a steaming, airless Black Maria to appear before a Kangaroo Court, dubbed a Special Military Tribunal where the proceedings leave no doubt at all that the judgement has been written in advance. And a sentence of death against which there is no appeal is a certainty.

Fearful odds? Hardly. The men who ordain and supervise this show of shame, this tragic charade are frightened by the word, the power of ideas, the power of the pen; by the demands of social justice and the rights of man. Nor do they have a sense of history. They are so scared of the power of the word, that they do not read. And that is their funeral.

When, after years of writing, I decided to take the word to the streets to mobilize the Ogoni people, and empower them to protest the devastation of their environment by Shell, and their denigration and dehumanization by Nigeria's military dictators, I had no doubt where it could end. This knowledge has given me strength, courage and cheer and given me psychological advantage over my tormentors.

Only yesterday, the Spirit of Ogoni magicked into my cell a lovely poem by Jack Mapanje, the veteran of Kamuza Banda's jails. Four years without charge, I had met Jack in person in Potsdam in 1992 and wondered how he had survived it all. Writing from Leeds University, his poem urged me to wear the armour of humour. The note at the end was also signed by Chengerai Hove, the award-winning Zimbabwean novelist. How wonderful to know how many fine men, the best brains, care for one's distress.

And yes, there has been humour along the way. At noon, on the 16th of March, 1995, my arch enemies, Shell, and the Nigerian government met at the Northumberland offices of the Nigerian High Commission. They had some interesting consensus. Shell had not been paid for four months. The High Commissioner promised they would be paid. The High Commissioner, nettled by the endeavours of Anita and Gordon Roddick on behalf of Ken Saro-Wiwa and the Ogoni people, devised 'ulterior motives' (such as a coup d'etat against the latest Nigerian military dictator, you know) and wondered how Shell could help with 'counter measures'. Shell assured the unhappy men that they were up to the antics of the 'propagandists', and were scoring successes. Shell was making its own film which would balance the films commissioned on the Ogoni by Channel 4. Shell had even succeeded in convincing some campaigners of the rightness of its cause. The High Commissioner, pleased by that development, urged that the Shell film be screened before the Channel 4 film being produced by Catma Films. He promised to assist Shell 'overcome any bureaucratic problems they may encounter in producing the films'. Shell reminded the High Commissioner how one Mr Boele had pretended to travel to Nigeria as a tourist but used the opportunity to conduct his research and interviews with various groups and individuals. The lesson, beware of human rights activists masquerading as tourists. Do not grant them visas. But please, the Nigerian government must pay Shell because 'lack of payment often leads to unemployment and unrest'. Meeting ended.

Thus the conspirators. Nothing about ending the genocide of the Ogoni, the trumped-up charges of murder against Ogoni leaders, the widespread misery caused to the Ogoni by the conspiratorial efforts of Shell and successive Nigerian military dictators. Just money and how to deflect concerned public opinion.

Ultimately, however, the fault lies at the door of the British government. It is the British government which supplies arms on CREDIT to the military dictators of Nigeria knowing full well that all such arms will only be used against innocent, unarmed citizens. It is the British government which makes noises about democracy in Nigeria and Africa but supports military dictators to the hilt. It is the British government which supports the rape and devastation of the environment by a valued tax-paying, labour-employing organisation like Shell. I lay my travails, the destruction of the Ogoni and other peoples in the Niger Delta at the door of the British government. Ultimately, the decision is for the British people, the electorate, to stop this grand deceit, this double standards which has lengthened the African nightmare and denigrates humanity.

Whether I live or die is immaterial. It is enough to know that there are people who commit time, money and energy to fight this one evil among so many others predominating worldwide. If they do not succeed today, they will succeed tomorrow. We must keep on striving to make the world a better place for all of mankind. Each one contributing his bit, in his or her own way.

I salute you all.
Ken Saro-Wiwa
12/5/95

Dear Eagle,

I got your notes on the discussions with BA [Brian Anderson of Shell]. Surprising that you should spend three hours making no progress. That Shell can be thinking of token measures in Ogoni shows that they are still not aware of the depth of their problems. Even their discussion with the Nigerian High Commission in London 16/3/95 shows that they are only interested in getting their money. They said nothing whatsoever about doing something about Ogoni, only to produce more films to counter the Ogoni campaign publicity. They still do not realize that the propaganda war was lost since 1993. Their PR dept. is out of touch with reality. When the minutes of the meeting gets to the Campaigning Group, Shell must blush.

Every day we spend in detention enhances the Ogoni cause and puts Shell on the block. So, detention is not a bad thing for us as such. I always knew that it was part of the struggle. Even death will only make me a martyr and enhance the cause.

I am surprised that Shell should be talking of trust and goodwill. If they had listened to me early in 1993, all this would not have arisen. It would have cost them far less. Anyway, I am looking for solutions, not trying to cast blame. Look at the following scenarios:

1. We remain in Jail. (A) The cause grows: Junior's recent visit to the US was a smasher. He met Al Gore, Ethel Kennedy, The Sierra Club, The World Bank, The Environmental Defence Fund, Trans Africa, The Political Director of US Oil, Chemical and Atomic Workers Union and the TGWA and the Commission on Environmental Strategy and Planning. Along with the Goldman Foundation, Shell could be facing an expensive call for the boycott of its products. The Canadian trip was equally useful and many promises were made.
(B) Within Nigeria, the other oil producing areas who have been watching to see if MOSOP's non-violent stand will

draw Shell out of its cocoon, decide that force is what Shell wants. There will be trouble on the oilfields, losing Shell a lot of its investment. Military force will not secure them peace on the oilfields. Everyone knows that now. As to the 'Major Environmental Survey', it will solve few problems if it does not have the support of the authentic community leaders or if Shell tries to play politics with it.

In the end all this could be *extremely* expensive for Shell particularly if as being mooted, we sue them in the US. Punitive damages could be imposed on them. Our sponsors are thinking in that direction. Is this what Shell wants?

OR THIS?

2. Shell uses its considerable clout to:
   i. Create an Ogoni State. We will have something to show the Ogoni people and assuage their anger.
   ii Shell gets the Tribunal stopped or the Federal Attorney General to enter a *nolle prosequi* using the fact of my ill health and inability to get on with the trial. Shell's stock in Ogoni rises. The human rights and writers lobbies which have stood solidly behind us abroad are disarmed. Shell gets a breathing space.
   iii. Ogoni is only 32 miles by 12. With the confidence the people have in me, we can work to get whatever compensation is due settled over a period of time. But Shell would have to ensure that the Fed. Govt. pays rents and royalties to land lord communities. I can convince the Ogoni people to lower their demands, although I would have to be extremely careful before they lynch me. Even the Govt. would welcome the better image this would create for them.

If I were Shell, I would prefer the second scenario. If they don't have direct access to Bully (but I don't believe that) they can work through the British High Commission. Bully relies on the BHC. And they can get anything from him.

With us busy on Ogoni affairs, Shell will find respite on the rest of the delta area while I remain in jail, I am a symbol of all the oil producing areas.

Time is of the essence in these matters. The campaign abroad is widening and is likely to move to Australia soon. In any case, the Sierra Club is determined to secure the best for the Ogoni.

You may show this letter to BA [Brian Anderson of Shell] and I pray he listens to us. And acts quickly. In the interest of Shell. Shell are the ones who need to show trust and goodwill. They have screwed Ogoni enough in the past.

Regards,
Ken

EAGLE
(Urgent)

* * *

Dear Mandy,

I got your note last night and I am hurrying this to you. You may edit it. The record of the meeting between Shell and the Nigerian government is available with my son. Keep smiling. God loves you.

Ken

* * *

8th June 1995
London, UK

Dear Junior,

Many thanks for the computer, the honey and video diskettes. Also the papers which came through. It's all served to lower my temperature, my anxiety. The January 1995 statement of account was missing, though you will please send it at an opportune moment.

It's no use worrying about my health. The barbarians out here do not want me to get medical care. And there is no question of their releasing me in order that I may get proper medical attention. I do not feel any worse than I have felt in the recent past, although mental torture and stress have affected me badly. Have no anxieties on this score. I believe that I will be alright, no matter how long this lasts.

The last I heard of the manuscripts I sent you, you were having problems with the diskettes. Have you sorted out the problem and sent the MS to the agent?

How did Gian fare on June 1? He's a major source of my worries.

I noticed that up to the end of April, the payments from Canada PEN and the Goldman Environmental Foundation had not been credited to the account. Please confirm that they are reflected in the May statement of account.

An Ogoni delegation consisting of members of the bereaved families and other politicians appears to be in Europe or should be there soon. I do not know exactly what their mission is but it would appear that they are to visit all those countries where I've won awards (to tell them to withdraw the awards, maybe!). The federal government may be using them for propaganda purposes but I doubt that they will be much use. The publicity was won long ago. It may be worth the while keeping a tab on them.

Professor Ake may be passing through London in a few days time on his way from the US. Please let him have the novel *Onrika*. I had thought that Comfort would bring it along.

You may have heard that I've been awarded the 8th Bruno Krelsky Human Rights Award 1995. The citation compares me with Mandela who won the same prize in 1981. The Award ceremony will be held in Vienna on September 29. I hope that you will be able to represent me.

I hope that your *Guardian* interview is successful and that you can settle into a job and a career. If it proves so, I'll be really happy. And, of course, I'll be happy you'll be getting out of sports into news. It's not that sports is bad, but it's really entertainment and our situation is too dire for our best people to be merely entertaining others.

I was pleased to hear from Noo at long last. I kept wondering what happened to her other letters. Let Zina know that I'm as excited about her Brazilian trip as she is and am looking forward to hearing how it goes. I hope that they have now both received the pocket money I sent them.

I am enclosing a letter to Alhaji Abubakar Alhaji, the Nigerian High Commissioner in London. You will please call him and say you have a private letter from me to him to be delivered personally by you. Read the letter carefully so that you can discuss with him and bring me back a message, if any.

My love to you and Olivia.

Jeje

P.S. Tell Lazarus Temana that we've received their letter and that I thank them. We will be sending a new scholarship list soon. I think they're doing a wonderful job.

By the way, your adopted name sounds funny in Khana and hasn't gone down well with the people here. There's no Khana way Ken Wiwa can be the son of Ken Saro-Wiwa. I hope you stick by Ken Saro-Wiwa Jnr in future. Gian could change to Gian Wiwa, you cannot.

Jeje

* * *

To Jack Mapanje
York, UK
20 May 1995

Dear Jack,

I received with great cheer the lovely poem you sent on 26th April. A million thanks. You have been much on my mind lately, following the news of our beloved friend, Hastings Kamuzu Banda, who did us the favour of locking you away for four years! Without the bother of a trial. I was most heartened that justice finally caught up with him and his associates. A lesson there for many who copy him or would want to do so. But do they ever learn?

Oh yes. Potsdam. You remember telling us how your captors marvelled at the great number of letters they received on your behalf. It took all of four years for these words to reach their hearts of stone, their millipede brains. Well, I've got news for you. The armed bandits here, driven by their greed for the evil of my beautiful Ogoni homeland, are acting even more deaf, and are they bloodthirsty! Time will also catch up with them.

I find comfort in what International PEN and all you good men and women out there are doing for me and my colleagues and I cannot tell you how pleased the Ogoni people are about it.

You urge me to laughter, courage and cheer. I have them in abundance. The 'eternal monsters' caught me in the evening of my life – when one sees death more clearly. They weren't smart enough to stop my dreams. This junta in love with old men.

My regards to Chengerai Hove. Tell him I still laugh at his compatriot who asked for multicultural coffee.

I wonder if Murtala Bakhari is still at Leeds? Give him my regards. My classmate H O Maduaka . . . was supposed to be on a sabbatical out there and I wonder if you were able to . . .

Best wishes from,
Yours sincerely,
(Signed) Ken Saro-Wiwa

* * *

Sister Majella McCarron
Dublin. Ireland
8 July 1995

Dear Sister M,

I got your diary of 5/5 to 16/6, and many thanks. As you never tell me which of my letters you have got and which you have not, I can only hope that you got all the letters I have sent you. Like you, I only hope that my letters do arrive.

185

I did get the book, GETTING TO YES, and many thanks for it. You must have known that the exploratory talks with Shell petered out even before they began. I have a feeling that Shell thinks they can sit all this out and carry on as before. I think they are wrong. All it means is that we have to work harder. It may even work in our favour that we do not negotiate just now, but that the situation in the country goes bad enough to make a total resolution of the contradictions necessary. In which case, we will also be negotiating for other peoples who are not up to it at this moment.

You know of the Niger Delta Environmental Survey. Claude Ake sits on its Steering Committee, representing the 'stake-holders' and has, indeed, held two meetings with us here in the detention camp. He confirms what we all knew: that Shell had wanted to do a 'greenwash'. However, it does appear that they won't be getting their way, it being that Claude is very clear as to what should happen, and is receiving support from one other member of the Committee – the chap from the World Conservation Fund who comes in from London and who is determined to ensure that his organisation is not misused by Shell. There is a stakeholders meeting in Port Harcourt, 24th to 26th August and I will let you know what goes on there. In the meantime, could you please check with Glenn if it's true that the Head of the Environmental Division of Shell at the Rotterdam office resigned rather than be a part of the grand deception which Shell planned instituting the Survey? The position paper appears to have sought for a way of using the survey to create communal dissension and for buying over local leaders. Check this out please.

Just as you were leaving for Rome, Dr Leton and Dr Birabi were flown to London by the federal government to try to undo some of the publicity the Ogoni campaign had put out. It would appear that Shell hosted them to dinner but I cannot say that they met with much more success than that. Ojukwu was on that same trip but I understand that they were booed when they spoke to their first audience and their first press conference was similarly a failure. The behaviour of the Ogoni politicians has been roundly condemned at home.

The trial has been adjourned to July 31. Our lawyers have now withdrawn and the Legal Aid Council of Rivers State has provided a lawyer for each of us. They now need to obtain all the proceedings and study them before the trial can recommence. We expect that they will get the proceedings from the Tribunal but we are not giving them any of our own papers. In short, we will not be co-operating with any of the defence counsel. We would like it known that the state are judge, prosecuting and defence counsel all rolled into one so that the true intent of the state is no longer masked.

Our lawyers withdrew after the Tribunal ruled that the failure of government to produce a video-cassette and transcripts of a press conference addressed by the military administrator and one of the prosecuting witnesses a day after the murders, was 'reasonable'. The government said they had wiped all the tapes for lack of funds. But they had in fact distributed the same throughout Nigeria and their embassies abroad in an attempt to calumniate me. So much for the trials.

The situation around us in the detention camp is a lot more relaxed now. 'Delta Force' forced Okuntimo out of his positions as Camp Commandant and Commander of the Internal Security Task Force and he has now been thrown to a harsh position in Minna. Consequently, we are now in ostensibly more civilised hands, although this is only relatively speaking. For a greasing of palms (you cannot avoid that in Nigeria – everyone's trading), people have access to us and can spend thirty minutes to one hour. This has been most relieving.

We have met with the youths and some of Ogoni, and have been able to get more accurate pictures of what is happening at home. The military harassment has been most frightening, and most people are scared to death. It has been impossible to hold meetings, and it does appear that the only meeting that is currently being held once a month is that summoned by my mother. She is patron of the organisation – BIAKA

(GLORIOUS WOMEN) – and the last meeting will be held on August 1 and I will be arranging for a video of that. I will also encourage them to watch 'Delta Force' and 'Drilling Fields'. They are surely in the vanguard of the resistance. I feel so proud of my mother! And she does it all so naturally! She's always at the Tribunal. So also my father who spent more than an hour with me here in prison a few days ago.

The men and the youths who seem to be the target of the military are more wary, but I expect that now that they have access to us, we will be able to motivate them. It is sad that all those whom we were training are now underground or in detention. This has left the people leaderless and I am worried that should this go on much longer, we may lose momentum. However we are now trying to encourage a new leadership, but this is not going to be easy. The harsh economic condition has placed too many burdens on people and resistance in the circumstances, especially where government is so very powerful, is a clear difficulty. We need a lot of money to organize the people, support those who are underground or are detained and pay legal fees. I must tell you that I've been under considerable pressure but I'm soldiering on with great faith in God and in my ultimate destiny.

I believe that settlement will come with the resolution of the national crisis. In that sense, the recent coup trials which have outraged the international community are welcome. The point, though, is will the world watch hands akimbo as they did in Idi Amin's Uganda while the best men are murdered? I fear that that might be the case, as the people in government who should act on these things are normally moved by every consideration but the preservation of human rights. More so when the crimes are committed against people in the Third World and commercial and industrial interests are involved. Zaire comes readily to mind.

I did receive a laptop computer from Junior through my younger sister, Comfort, the Zaria-based lawyer who was in Britain for a fortnight or so. This has eased my pain a great deal, and am beginning to write again, after a lull of seven months. Seven wasted months! I'm encouraging Ledum and John Kpuinen to also learn how to use the computer so they can keep themselves busy.

You will be telling me about your month-long stay in Rome in your next letter, no doubt. And also let me know how you settle into your new situation. I can't just reconcile myself to the fact that we will not be seeing you in Ogoni again, at least not in the foreseeable future. But then, I'm not in Ogoni either. What is comforting is that you are well and that you will always be in touch, quite apart from the fact that spiritually, we are together.

I got the photographs of the march, and was very pleased to see your seraphic person looking tense in one or two of them. Some lawyer from Ledum's chambers grabbed them to make photocopies so, as I write, I've not really had time to look at them closely. I'll do so in due course.

Please give my regards to members of Ogoni Solidarity Ireland and say how grateful we are for their care and concern. Also give my thanks to Mairead Corrrigan. I cannot believe that anyone should think me fit to receive the Nobel Prize for Peace. I also hate to think that I've not been able to travel to receive any of the prizes I've won save the Fonlon-Nichols award. The joy lies in the recognition. To think that I should be the Nigerian with the greatest number of international awards. And that I should be an Ogoni! What's that about the stone rejected by the builders? God is good, as we say over here.

I must stop here and wish you the best of luck. I look forward to hearing from you soon.

Sincerely,
Ken

* * *

Anon
To Ken
'And now these three remain; faith, hope and love. But the greatest of these is love'.

1 Corinthians 13. v 13.

'Love is patient, love is kind. It does not envy, it does not boast, it is not proud. It is not rude, it is not self-seeking. It is not easily angered, it keeps no record of wrongs. *Love does not delight in evil but rejoices with the truth. It always protects, always trusts, always hopes, always perseveres. Love never fails'*.

1 Corinthians 13. v 4-8.

* * *

[This was the last recorded letter from Ken Saro-Wiwa]

14th September 1995

Dear Sister Majella,

Many thanks for your letters up to the end of July or thereabouts. I believe that I've got everything you have sent thus far. Some of them came rather late and out of sequence, but I do get them. Because I keep them around me just to read and re-read them, I've had two of them seized lately. I hope that I will get them back, anyway, some day.

I expect that you have now started your new assignment and am really happy for you. It is hard to think that you will no longer be with us here in Nigeria, but it may well be that we shall be better served by your being away. God works in mysterious ways his wonders to perform.

You have heard of the raid on my office of July 29. That was followed by a raid on our cells in the prison a week or so later. Since the departure of Okuntimo [in charge of the Internal Security Task Force] on July 1, and indeed long before then, for Okuntimo suddenly lost interest in punishing us thanks to the education we gave him, security had eased a great deal and we were able to receive a host of visitors from Ogoni and elsewhere. I'm sorry to say that we became lax ourselves and so when the new man struck, we 'lost' quite a lot of property.

190

Back to business. The trial is being speeded up. Which means that every rule is being broken in order that it might end. I expect that it will end before you get this letter. I have information that judgment will not be delivered, which will mean that we will remain in prison for as long as the authorities please, keeping me out of circulation for as long as Abacha is in power.

I am not defending myself I will want to make a Statement. I have already filed the Statement at the High Court here and a copy is available with my son in London, if you want to read it. It is possible that the Judge will not allow me to read it, but it is already a public document and the press can use it.

About a week ago, Major Obi Umahi (an Igbo) who now commands the ISTF came to me and asked what he could do to ensure peace in Ogoni. I asked him to release the three Ogoni activists who were arrested after the raid on my office, and use them to speak to the Ogoni people. He promptly released them from detention at Afam the next day and brought them to my cell. He then sought my blessing on the peace effort he meant to launch. I gave that blessing after drawing his attention to the fact that there are three parties involved in the matter: the Ogoni people, Shell and the Government (State and Federal). I did not mind where he started from, I said, so long as he realised that peace could only come when justice is done.

As of now, a core group is being widened to include the disaffected politicians. The hope, I gather, is that the Ogoni people can be made to come together to defend Ogoni interests. I don't know that anyone can reconcile the skulduggery of Leton and Birabi with the rest of the people. My assumption is that government are preparing the ground for the conviction of Ledum and myself – to ensure that the Ogoni do not riot when the inevitable verdict long decided upon is handed down.

Yesterday the ground was cleared for that conviction when the no-case submission made by the Legal Aid lawyers was dismissed. The Tribunal said: 'The prosecution adduced evidence of the killing of four chiefs of Giokoo through civil disturbances there by NYCOP youths. There is evidence of the leadership of MOSOP who by meetings, rallies, provocative and instigative pronouncements light (sic) the fuse that produced the consuming events of 21/5/94 at Gbenmene Palace, Giokoo'. Whoever was in doubt knows where the Tribunal is heading to. The stories below are for your entertaimnent.

By July 1, Okuntimo and Komo [Military Administrator of Rivers State] were at daggers drawn. I believe Komo finally saw through the brute he had appointed to supervise the decimation of the Ogoni and knew he had made costly mistakes. As usual with the military, he could not apologise to us; in any case, his career was already on the line. All he could do was persist in evil.

The Federal Government were shamed at the last meeting of the UN Committee for the Eradication of Racial Discrimination (CERD) attended on our behalf by Barika and on the government side by a team which included George Kobani (as consultant), the Legal Adviser to Abacha, a Professor Yadudu (Yahoo!) and Ambassador Azikiwe (second son of the great Zik). The government delegation declared me guilty of murder (!) and the Committee felt that since they were denying all the assertions made by the various human rights groups, they might as well go to Ogoni to see for themselves. I doubt that they will be coming, but I wish it would happen. A newspaper here published an item stating that Shell has been pressuring the government to create an Ogoni State and give the oil committees 50 per cent of oil revenues. Shell has not denied this item, and there may be some truth in it.

Ogoni is buzzing with all sorts of noises, all sorts of expectation. The first meeting aimed at reconciliation was held yesterday (13th) the date on which our defence opened. I believe that government will be told that peace in Ogoni depends also on all those now held in detention or driven underground being free. They won't listen to that. I can only hope that our conviction does not lead to more trouble. I have tried to bring home to all the example of Christ which was, to our people, fictional, I guess. They are now going to learn a hard lesson and I hope they take it quietly. I will keep you posted as events unravel. The ways of this struggle have been so unpredictable, I don't know what to say. There is an unseen hand at work. We are just not in control, and no one seems to be. It's amazing the things which do happen! I must thank you and all those who have done so much work for us abroad. It's nice to know that people who have worked or visited Ogoni are now turning up and lending assistance in various ways. The commitment of Anita Roddick is a great blessing. It has nettled the Nigerian High Commissioner in London, for one!

I am in good spirits, expecting the worst as usual, but hopeful for the best. My parents are always in court, and my father believes that I will be free at the end of the case. I've tried very hard to dampen his optimism but the old man won't budge. I just hope he does not get a rude shock.

One source of worry is what will happen to our struggle when Ledum and I are put away. We had not had enough time to train the cadres or put alternative leaderships in place. And putting members of the Steering Committee on the police wanted list has deprived us of a lot of hands. I have been able to direct things and even contribute to the publicity war from detention. I don't know if I'll be able to do so from prison. We have no funds, not even a bank account. Everything had hinged so much upon my resources that my absence will cause a lot of problems. We'll have to get around that somehow.

Don't be embarrassed by my ocean of ink. I am not. I'm only tired now and must go to bed, to rise early and prepare for the boredom of the Tribunal.

Regards,
Ken

For Sister Majella McCarron

Sister M, my sweet soul sister,
What is it, I often ask, unites
County Fermanagh and Ogoni?
Ah, well, it must be the agony
The hunger for justice and peace
Which married our memories
To a journey of faith.
How many hours have we shared
And what oceans of ink poured
From fearful hearts beating together
For the voiceless of the earth!
Now, separated by the mighty ocean
And strange lands, we pour forth
Prayers, purpose and pride
Laud the integrity of ideals
Hopefully reach out to the grassroots
Of your Ogoni, my Fermanagh.

Ken Saro-Wiwa
20/6/95

Letters to Ken Saro-Wiwa's family and condolence notes after 10 November 1995

Office of the President of South Africa

25 November 1995

Mrs Saro-Wiwa
Care of Archbishop Tutu

Dear Mrs Saro-Wiwa

I have asked Archbishop Tutu to bring to you this expression, on my own behalf and on behalf of the Government of National Unity of South Africa, of our heartfelt condolences on your tragic loss.

The cruel and callous execution of Ken Saro-Wiwa, along with the other eight activists for Ogoni rights, outraged us all. For me personally it was a deep shock, and a bitter disappointment that our efforts and those of others had failed to avert this terrible deed.

We know that for you and your family, the pain is deep. But please know that we share your grief and that our thoughts are with you. Be assured that the example of Ken's courage will fortify us in our resolve to work for the restoration of democracy in Nigeria.

Yours sincerely,
Nelson Mandela
President

* * *

Office of the Prime Minister of New Zealand

14 November 1995

Mr Ken Wiwa
London

Dear Mr Wiwa

I write on behalf of all New Zealanders to express our deep sadness and shock at the tragic death of your father. Please accept my and the New Zealand Government's most sincere condolences. Your father made a significant contribution to the Ogoni people during his lifetime, and it was a tragedy that someone of such talent had his life cut short in this way.

I was deeply distressed that my appeal to General Abacha for clemency was ignored, along with appeals by others in the international community. I and my Commonwealth colleagues shared a deep sense of outrage at the action of the Nigerian authorities. I was pleased to meet you in Auckland and had hoped for a happier outcome to your visit to New Zealand and Commonwealth pleas on your father's behalf. Tragically that did not happen.

My thoughts and prayers are with you and your family at this difficult time.

Yours sincerely

Rt Hon J B Bolger
Prime Minister

* * *

Office of the Prime Minister of Canada

November 11, 1995.

Dear Mr Wiwa:

I would like to express to you and to your family my deep condolences and those of the Government and people of Canada on the death of your father. I know how badly you must feel. The hope we held when we met yesterday that he might be saved was in vain.

His execution, and that of the other eight Ogoni who had been sentenced to death, is a tragedy and a travesty of justice.

I want to assure you that Canada, and I am certain, the Commonwealth, will clearly express their outrage. You can be assured of our own sentiment in this regard.

In this difficult time for you personally, you can be confident that your activities on behalf of justice and democracy in Nigeria have made a difference.

Yours sincerely,
Jean Chrétien

Mr Ken Wiwa
C/o Ogoni Foundation
LONDON, UK

* * *

Fax from Anita and Gordon Roddick,
Founders of The Body Shop

To Maria Saro-Wiwa
Ken Saro-Wiwa

12 November 1995.

Dear Maria, Ken and family,
   Anita and I arrived in the USA and heard the dreadful news
when we landed, we are completely devastated by the
brutality of this heinous crime. The evening I spent with Ken
when he laughed so humorously at the High Commissioner,
that vile criminal, stands out in my mind. Our hearts and
thoughts are with you as you grieve. Ken was and is an
inspiration to both of us personally – he is and will remain a
hero, a shinning example of courage and selflessness.
   You must be inundated with messages of support and
condolence. Please do not hesitate to ask us for help when you
need it. We are constantly thinking of you and your whole
family. Our house is your home as long as you need it.

   Gordon and Anita Roddick

* * *

Ethel Kennedy (widow of Bobby Kennedy)
Virginia, US

Dearest Ken,

How often in the past weeks I have paused to put my arms around you.

The tears of the world are mixed with your own and the cries of anguish are heard above all the music of Heaven.

Reading the lines from 'I Think Continually of Those who Were Truly Great' so remind me of Jack and Bobby, and, now, your Dad: Three heroic hearts.

'Near the snow, near the sun in the highest fields, see how their names are feted by the highest grass'.

And by the streamers of white clouds.

And whispers of wind in the listening sky.

The names of those who in their lives, fought for life. Who wore at their hearts the fires centre.

Born of the sun, they travelled a short while toward the sun and left the vivid air signed with their honor.'

Ken – your wonderful father will remain forever in my daily prayers.

With love,
Ethel

* * *

The English Centre of INTERNATIONAL PEN
A WORLD ASSOCIATION OF WRITERS
London, UK

14/11/95

Ken Wiwa
The Ogoni Foundation
London, UK

Dear Ken Wiwa,

It is with a heavy heart that I write to you today, but, at the same time the recognition that the spirit of your father, Ken Saro-Wiwa, will live on and on. It is not only for the Ogoni people that he has become a hero, for all of us, and perhaps, particularly, for fellow writers round the world, he is now an emblem of International PEN's charter, the defence of freedom of speech for all.

On a personal note, we think of your loss, of your sorrow, and how one cannot replace a father. May I tell you a little story? On Saturday I went to Oxford to see my grandson – aged 14 – play Rugby against a neighbouring school; he from St. Edward's (known as Teddys), and the opposing team, Abingdon. In my grandson's team, there was a Nigerian boy, giving his all to the team. Afterwards, James (my grandson) told me that they were all being very caring towards this boy on that day as he had received the news that his uncle had been hung, in Nigeria. So you will understand from this that the news of the hanging reached down to the youngest among us. James was very sad for the boy, as were his colleagues. But the evil happening has struck the developing generation as something outside the pail of their understanding, and, as the Foreign Office said to PEN when we did our first demonstration outside the Nigerian High Commission: 'You are beginning to annoy the Nigerian High Commission, KEEP IT UP!'

I believe you have visited our English PEN centre, and now

I would suggest that you do so again, because, as you may sense when you come, English PEN who began the PEN idea sixty years ago, is the nucleus of a very large family – 96 countries in all – this family supporting each other when possible.

I have to find out more about the Nigerian schoolboy because his uncle could have been any of the nine Nigerians hung.

Our warmest wishes to you and your family, our support and our admiration and the sympathy for all that you must be suffering at this present time.

Yours sincerely,
Pauline Neville
Chairman of the Books to Writers In Prison Committee.

* * *

20 November 1995   Adeline Koh
                                                    Malaysia

Mr Ken Wiwa
London, UK

Dear Sir,

I send greetings to you from Malaysia and I wish to express my grief to you and your family of the news of your father. I also send my condolences to the family of the other men executed along with your father for the cause they believed in.

I personally stand for the rights and justice of your people and I wish to contribute to that cause from my country. I wish to make a stand on your behalf to the government of my country and against Shell Trading Sdn. Bhd, in Kuala Lumpur. Please write to me that I can take action.

Apart from the action taken by The Body Shop, the company I serve, I choose to make further contributions for you and your people. May this injustice and affliction come to an end very soon and may your father's ideas live forever.

Thank you.
Yours sincerely,
Adeline Koh

Alex Wright
Los Angeles, USA

Ken Saro-Wiwa
Ogoni Community Association UK
London, UK

November 13th 1995

Dear Ken,

I was very sorry to hear about your Dad's death. It was on the front page of the *LA Times* yesterday. It is really shocking.

I did not know your Dad, but he must have been incredibly brave and strong to face up to the Nigerian government.

I know you have been lobbying to get your Dad released these past few months. I cannot even imagine how you must feel.

Liz and I both send our love to you. If there is anything we can do for you, please let us know.

Love,

Alex

[Alex Wright is an old school friend of Ken Wiwa]

* * *

Cheam Hawtreys
Berkshire, UK

November 16, 1995.

Dear Maria,

The events of the past week have distressed us all greatly, and Chris and I particularly have been thinking of you and the family so much. We have managed to see all the recent programmes on television, and watching Ken on Tuesday night made us remember him again as we knew him – the big smile through the haze of pipe smoke. Chris remembers the many times that they chatted on the touch-line or boundary (both puffing their pipes!) watching Tedum perform so magnificently, and it was with this in mind that Chris was able to remember with such meaning last Sunday.

All our thoughts are with you and your family at this time – and you must be very proud of Ken Jr. Your girls must have left Roedean by now and are no doubt pursuing successful University careers.

If you find yourself anywhere near Cheam, and would like to drop in for a visit, please do – just let us know you are coming so that we can be certain to be here. The enclosed appeared in the Newbury paper this week.

Our love to you all,

Chris and Penny

* * *

Cutting enclosed with letter reads:

School remembers Saro-Wiwa

Ken Saro-Wiwa was remembered as a 'happy, fun-loving man,' by Christopher Evers, the headmaster of Cheam Hawtreys preparatory school, Headley, this week. Mr Saro-Wiwa was a regular visitor to the school when his late son, Tedum, was a pupil there between 1986 and 1991. When Tedum died of a heart condition in 1993, Mr Evers gave a funeral address at Eton. Mr Evers said 'Ken Saro-Wiwa was only five feet, four inches tall but he was a large, bubbly character, a very amusing, human sort of guy. He used to come down and puff his pipe on the edge of the field, watching Tedum play'. At Sunday's Remembrance Day service at the school, Mr Evers paid tribute to Mr Saro-Wiwa as 'a fighter for freedom', a man who died fighting for a cause. Tedum Saro-Wiwa was one of the most outstanding sportsmen in Cheam Hawtrey's history, an outstanding cricketer, who also excelled at rugby and football. When he died, pupils at the school mounted a display of photographs, cuttings and personal reflections in his memory.

* * *

East London Partnership
UK

13 November 1995

Personal
Olivia Burnett
Prince of Wales Business Leaders Forum

Dear Olivia,

This is one of those letters you hope you never have to write.

I was terribly sad to hear of Ken's father's death on Friday. It must be so much worse when the world's press is tramping over private grief. Words are not always a comfort at times like these, but I hope you will feel a little better in knowing that your friends have you in their thoughts.

The enclosed Auden poem is still wonderfully powerful, despite its over-exposure in 'Four Weddings...' It helps.

Finally, I enclose a wonderful photograph of you from Rio, which I happened on when Linden Longino dropped in today. For all the bad things in our world, there are the truly good.

With best wishes,
Tony Hawkshead

* * *

Ken Saro-Wiwa's only crime was to campaign for his people. The Nigerian military killed him for it.

On November 10, 1995 at 11.30 am, Ken Saro-Wiwa, Dr Barinem Kiobel, John Kpuinen, Barbrio Bera, Saturday Dobee, Felix Nwate, Nordu Eawo, Paul Levura and Daviel Bbokoo were executed by the Abacha Military Junta. They were Ogoni activists and members of the Movement for the Survival of the Ogoni People (MOSOP).

At this time, a further 29 Ogoni activists are in custody, threatened with the same fate.

Please lend your support to MOSOP, by contacting Frank Kirwan, Ogoni Solidarity Ireland, [http:/www.comhlamh.org/]

Bliain faoi Mhaise

This postcard is from Bliain faoi Mhaise, an Irish organisation which strongly supports the Ogoni cause. Members of this group, known as the Rossport 5, are currently in prison for protesting against attempts of Royal Dutch Shell to lay dangerous high-pressure raw gas pipelines in their ancient homeland, Bogs of Erris. Sister Majella writes in September 2005 'in the tradition of the Ogoni 9 and Ogoni 20, the people . . . began to call themselves the Bogoni.'

* * *

Writings from writers around the world on hearing about the brutal killing of Ken Saro-Wiwa and eight other Ogoni.

On his death:
'The death of Saro-Wiwa is only Nigeria's most recent wound. And she will receive many more until she is delivered from a dictatorship so contemptuous of the well-being of her people and of world opinion'.
Chinua Achebe

'This shameful act of murder deprives Nigeria of one of her finest writers and International PEN will do all in its power to bring those responsible to account before the world'.
Ronald Harwood

'There are some things on Earth that are stronger than death, and one of these is the eternal human quest for justice... A writer in Nigeria was sentenced to death in the quest for a better life for his people. The consequence is incalculable'.
Ben Okri

The focus now should be on transforming Nigeria, and using this energy and this rage towards improving the conditions of the Nigerian people'.
Ben Okri

'This is Heart of Darkness country'.
Fay Weldon

'Nigeria is now on a similar level of moral degeneracy as Saddam Hussein's Iraq'.
William Boyd

'Murder is the most brutal form of censorship and the Nigerian military has proved by this act the desperation of its leaders who are prepared to take any steps to stay in power'.
Harold Pinter

'Once again greed has deprived human beings of the wisdom of someone who revered the earth. In our despair over the execution of Ken Saro-Wiwa, we must commit out lives both to controlling the need to steal from others that might arise in ourselves, and to acting in solidarity with anyone, anywhere, who stands for the right of people and the planet to live in dignity'.
Alice Walker

'He and his colleagues did not die because of literary output, but as a result of their fight for the Ogoni people's survival and against the tyranny of the Abacha regime. That fight must now become the world's fight'.
Salman Rushdie

'We condemn this immoral act. The outrage of the literary community will reverberate for years to come, and we will do our utmost to ensure that the government of Nigeria is made to feel the consequences of its heinous behaviour'.
Joint statement by Arthur Miller and Susan Sontag

Writings for Ken Saro-Wiwa

Warm thoughts for Ken Saro-Wiwa

I was beginning to recover from the grisly
Gecko that burst on the blanket rags of my
Knees, after severing from the cobweb rafters
Of my Mikuyu Prison recess, when I heard

The armed vultures have snatched you again;
My heart aches. I remember your gentle embrace
At Potsdam to salute my release from another
Choking cell; you recalled the freezing breath

That writers globally sprayed on the lion's balls
To loosen its flesh-clutching jaws; I bragged about
Fleas and swarms of bats pouring stinking shit
Into our mouths as we battled the eternal monsters

Of our wakeful slumbers; you laughed. Today
You must invoke that humour again, my brother:
And as we marvel at those handcuff scars darkly
Glistening, courage. Watch the cracks on your

Prison walls, let them nimbly hold the razors and
Needles of the life we once endured; let the rapture
Of gracious laughter shared, the memory of justice,
Succour you like a prayer; then as the countless

Scorpions, mosquitoes and cockroaches fuss about
Your walls, remember to reach out for that tender
Cloud which forever hovers above your solitary
Sanctum with our wishes to restore and to cheer.

Jack Mapanje, 1995

* * *

For Ken Saro-Wiwa

That he should be jailed
And tortured
For loving the land
The earth
And crying out at its
Defilement
Is monstrously unfitting
We live in unnatural times;
And we must make it
Natural again
With our wailing.

For unnatural times also become
Natural by tradition
And by silence.
That is why the lands
Today ring with injustice
With lies
With prejudice
Made natural.

The earth deserves our love.
Only the unnaturals
Can live so at ease
While they poison the land
Rape her for profit
Bleed her for oil
And not even attempt
To heal the wounds.

Only the unnaturals
Jail those whose loves are bold
Who are weepers of the earth's agony
Handmaidens of her quiet vengeance
Sybils of her future rage.
Only the unnaturals

Rule our lands today
So deal to the wailing
Of our skies, of the hungry,
Of the strange new diseases
And of that dying earth
Bleeding and wounded
And breeding only deserts
Where once there were
The proud trees of Africa
Cleaning their rich hair
In the bright winds of heaven.

That he should be jailed
For loving the land
And tortured
For protecting his people
And crying out
As the ancient town-criers did
At the earth's defilement
Is monstrously unfitting.
And we live in unnatural times.
And we must make it
Natural again
With our singing
And our intelligent rage

Ben Okri, 1995

* * *

PART IV
Fathers and Sons, 2000
A Letter to My Father, 2005
by Ken Wiwa

Fathers and Sons, 2000

Dear Jeje,

Someone once told me that when your father dies, he takes a little bit of you with him and leaves a little bit of himself in you. I have been trying to work out what you took and what you left, trying to establish where you end and where I begin. This is the final chapter in that process, and I still don't know where you end, but I know that I began on the night Felix was born and asked me a simple question.

When he was delivered, the midwife handed him to me. I wasn't expecting to get the first look, so I was completely unprepared. I'm sure you know how hard it is to describe your emotions when you see your son for the first time. You have anticipated the moment, tried to imagine what it will feel like; yet when it comes, it still takes you by surprise.

We stared at each other. I didn't know what to do or say. I suppose I was looking for signs of me in him, trying to confirm that he was my son. He looked as surprised as I was, but he had this intense, precocious little frown on his face. The question was in his eyes. "Who are you?"

I didn't understand why at the time, but that frown unnerved me, and it was months before I was able to look him squarely in the eyes.

Olivia's excited voice interrupted our first discussion.

"Is it a boy?"

"Erm, yes it is," I replied and handed him over without even checking.

Mother and son took to each other with an uncomplicated affection. I must admit I felt a twinge of jealousy. As I watched the doctor and midwife fussing over my family, I felt

I was intruding on an intimate moment. I slipped out of the room to make the announcements.

Nene was fast asleep in a waiting room outside the delivery ward. She took the news in her waking stride and told me she had just seen Felix in a dream. I smiled. I felt so proud. I led her into the delivery room. When she saw her grandson's little face, she melted and I saw her lovely smile for the first time in years. She stood by the bed, stroking Felix's head with such tenderness that I cried. It really was a bittersweet moment because I would have given anything for you and Tedum to be in that room with us.

Olivia and I chatted into the early hours, staring at the small human being we had brought into the world. I was pensive when I finally drove home. My thoughts drifted back to the moment Felix and I had our first conversation and it occurred to me that I didn't have an answer to my son's first question.

I couldn't sleep that night. I paced around, trying to make sense of the scattered thoughts swirling in my brain. I sat down at my computer and sent out some emails. I can't remember what I wrote, but it was something about waking from a bad dream to find that the sun was shinning and birds were still singing in the trees.

It's been more than three years now since that night, but it feels more like eighty-six because I have re-lived two lives since then – yours and mine.

I was just thinking that all this should be private, but I realise that you, of all people, would understand. That's the way it's always been with us: the personal is political. We sold our privacy to the public a long time ago. Anyway, to put you in the picture, I am in good spirits, and for once in my life I really feel I know where I am going. I'm lucky that I have been able to spend so much time with Felix; but it's been a mixed blessing because I've mostly been locked away in this room, writing, trying to find an answer to his question. I am writing this from my study, which is an annexe of my bedroom in our home in Toronto. There are pictures of Felix,

Suanu (your second grandson), Olivia, Nene and Tedum on my desk and on my walls. None of you, I'm afraid. I still get a little anxious when I catch you staring at me. I hope that feeling goes if and when I ever feel I've done you proud. Yet I don't need a picture of you in here, because I can sense you all around me anyway. I am looking at my fingers as I type and I'm still amazed at how *familiar* they are, how they bend at the same angles, how they peck at the keyboard just as yours used to do. Stubby little Wiwa fingers, these.

I have noticed that my face is changing too. Jeje, I am getting old, you know. It amazes me to think that I am *five years* older than you were when I was born. And yet I still think of myself as your son, a boy, hardly a man and a father. But the evidence on my face is unmistakable: look how I've put on weight! Because I've been fairly sedentary for the first time in my life, my face is fuller, a few more chins downstairs, and upstairs the hairline has already begun its inevitable retreat. I'm watching out for the moment I take a good, long look in the mirror and have to accept that the man staring back at me looks like my father.

If these 86 years have taught me anything, though, it is this: it is not just through physical appearance that parents reveal themselves in their children. I still maintain that I don't look exactly like you – there are enough traces of Nene in me to assuage those fears – but there are subtler signs of you in me. Like the study, for instance. There are the obvious items, such as the shelf of your books, but there are also the cabinets crammed full of documents in a neat filing system; and the venetian blinds that must have subliminally reminded me of the ones in your study when they chose me. Nene once saw me beavering away in here, and she said, "Junior, you're just like your father, you know?" She was smiling to herself as she said this. It was a coy, girlish smile, as if she were remembering the young man she fell in love with. The thing is, our lives do seem to be following an eerily similar trajectory. Our stories overlap and complement each other. Chinua Achebe once wrote that each generation regenerates the circumstances that created the previous generation. I suspect a genetic instruction behind our narratives, adding and subtracting, writing a new chapter to the Gbenedorbi saga whenever one chapter comes to an end.

My story, the struggle to find the beginning to my own chapter, is almost complete now, and I hope that in narrating mine, I have helped to tell a little bit of yours. I hope – in fact, I know – you would approve of the functionality of that, but there have been so many distractions. The interest in you and the struggle has been phenomenal. I seem to spend my life answering enquiries about you. The irony is that every time I throw myself into the task, I understand and appreciate you a little more.

I am fairly diligent when the mood takes me, but it is a thankless task. There are times when I feel as if I'm chasing my tail. It comes at me from all angles: post, email, telephone and fax. It started with the condolences, hundreds of them; letters, cards and faxes from every corner of the world. It was humbling and reassuring to see just how much you meant to people. I responded to all of them – just as you had always advised me to do. But that was in the first flush of enthusiasm. The letters, faxes, requests and proposals kept coming, and even though the influx has slowed, it hasn't stopped and probably never will.

I don't resent the imposition any more, though. No, handling the by-products of your life has become something of a labour of love for me. Managing your legacies is a full-time job, but I see myself as an unpaid volunteer, bonded by blood and inspired by both love and determination to honour and keep your memory alive.

I am conscious when I survey the mountains of paper in this room that buried in there are some of my own documents – stray pieces, but poignant reminders nevertheless that I have a life of my own. Every now and again, I hear the most important reminder loitering outside the door, trying to grab my attention. Your grandson has an uncomplicated and irresistible way of getting that attention – he just barges in and demands it.

I just hope he doesn't have to remind me too often of the day he came in here and I ignored him. He stood by the door, watched me trying to fulfil my duty to you. I could see him out of the corner of my eye as I typed away. When I didn't acknowledge him, he turned around and walked out quietly. My heart sank. I slumped back in my chair. He came back a few minutes later, though, and this time, I turned to face him as soon as he walked in. He had that intense, precocious little frown on his face, the same question in his eyes. I smiled at him and held his gaze. His eyes lit up and he ran into my arms, shouting: "Daddeee!"

Jeje, rest in peace.

Your Son

A Letter to My Father, 2005

Dear Jeje,

It still feels a little strange to be writing to you posthumously and in such a public place but I am getting used to this – our personal will always be political. But what I find so reassuring is that we can still communicate, and whenever we talk the great puzzle that is Ken Saro-Wiwa becomes a little clearer. Ken Saro-Wiwa has many important components but your letters, your books, the insights and the values they contain makes the job that little bit easier.

For sure, it is a politically charged legacy but not the least of it for me is the very personal need to finally lay your body to rest. I guess you knew that when you wrote: *On the Death of Ken Saro-Wiwa* and predicted that the goons would deny you 'six feet of earth'. I think more people should read you because your words, your life and death are pregnant with so much political meaning and have so often proved to be eerily prophetic.

Your death should, in retrospect, have been a salutary lesson in what happens when corporations rule our world; but few people really understood the significance of what happened on 10th November 1995 – *The Times* described your execution as a 'cautionary tale of the 20th century' and your friend, Chuks Illoegbunam, posed and answered his own question in the London *Guardian*: 'what does Ken Saro-Wiwa's death mean? It means nothing has changed.'

On reflection, I think Chuks' observation was actually a challenge; to his readers, to everyone who felt profoundly uneasy that a writer, who had prosecuted a just environmental cause on a non-violent platform, could be met with the indifference and hostility of a military dictatorship and a multinational, be sentenced to death by an illegally constituted court and then hanged before a world audience, despite international and diplomatic pleas for his life.

Ten years have passed and, despite all the public outrage and grief, it appears that the world hasn't learned anything from your death: we still live in a world where corporations rank profits well above their value to people and the planet. Our world remains one in which corporations can, and do, routinely get away with murder.

In our small way we continue to try to make them accountable – you will be happy to know that we did manage to bring a suit against Shell in the US for their role in your arrest, detention, trial and execution. They have been charged under the provisions of the Alien Torts Claims Act, the Torture Victim Protection Act, and the Racketeer Influenced and Corrupt Organisations (RICO) Act. And the case will, if nothing else, fulfil your prediction that 'Shell is here on trial. The company has, indeed, ducked this particular trial, but its day will surely come.'

Your prediction was uppermost in my mind when the Centre for Constitutional Rights advised that I could bring the multinational to court in the US for their role in your murder. But it has taken eight years of judicial arguments for the US courts to declare that Shell has a case to answer for their role in your murder.

All this legal to-ing and fro-ing reminds me of when you had high hopes that I would pursue a career in law. You know I resisted you for all kinds of reasons, but fundamentally I always thought it was too stereotypical of what every African wants for their children. I wanted to use my imagination but, having seen and better understood what happened to our people and to you, I now understand that a creative project for an African requires the imaginative use of every tool at our disposal – from business to science to art and to, of course, the law to free us from our predicament.

Our complaint against Shell was filed in 1996. It accuses them of crimes against humanity, torture, summary execution, arbitrary detention, and racketeering, alleging that their actions in Nigeria violate the provisions of the Alien Tort Claims Act.

It took six years of legal arguments and appeals, chiefly over jurisdiction, before Judge Kimba Wood declared in our favour on 28 February 2002, acknowledging that there was sufficient evidence of collusion between Shell and the Nigerian military to qualify as racketeering under the RICO Act.

As I write, the case has just finished the discovery stage and, from what I have observed, it seems Shell is more concerned about procedure and technicalities than the substantive allegations. It is sickening that a company with such resources, that is in a 'win-win' situation in Nigeria – an organisation that has earned billions from our land – remains unwilling to take responsibility for its actions and is trying to portray itself as an innocent bystander and even victim of unscrupulous, black Africans. Poor little rich Shell!

What really sticks in the craw is that last year they were found guilty of misrepresenting their proven reserves by as much as four billion barrels – in effect, selling a false prospectus to shareholders. You won't be surprised that much of the scandal happened within Shell's Nigerian subsidiary. When the Chairman of Shell International, Sir Philip Watts, – yes the same Philip Watts who was in charge of Shell Nigeria when they had you locked you up – resigned or was sacked (with a six figure bonus for his sins). The New York stock exchange responded swiftly and fined Shell. And, within a few days of the scandal breaking, those who had bought Shell stock on a false prospectus were busy filing lawsuits against the company. The market moves swiftly to protect investors yet when the same organization violates human rights and destroys the environment, it can take a generation to get redress.

That's the world your grandchildren will grow up in, and

there are times when I think it is better you left this world behind. But it could have been so different couldn't it?

I remember how excited you were when the Berlin Wall came down in 1989. I remember you saw it as an opportunity for our people finally to stand up for our rights because the world was encouraging minorities, especially in Eastern Europe, to stand up for theirs. You wrote that if it was good for the former countries of the Soviet Union, it was surely good for communities like the Ogoni. Trapped in post-colonial nation-states that cheated minorities like the Ogoni of our right to self-determination, no longer would African people be treated as strategic pawns in Cold War chess games, and we would benefit from the so-called peace dividend.

I remember those days too: it was a time when environmental awareness was high on the public agenda in the West, and the Second Earth Summit in Rio confirmed that a critical mass was building behind a desire to build a kinder, gentler world. Capitalism had overcome socialism and some people were even suggesting it was the end of history.

Imagine that ten years after the triumphalism of the West, we had apparently squandered the peace dividend, and there were anti-capitalism riots in Seattle, and the newspapers were full of headlines like 'capitalism in crisis'.

When I ask myself what went wrong, I think back to your murder, coming as it did in between the collapse of the Soviet Union and the Seattle riots. Looking back, your killing merely proved that unrestrained capitalism did not deliver higher standards of living for everyone, but actually contributed to greater inequalities of wealth, attendant public disorder and greater levels of human insecurity. The first Gulf War (1991) had already indicated that the New World Order was not new but reactionary; one that would go to any lengths to eliminate anything or anyone who threatened the *status quo* in the supply of energy. Your murder merely ratified that the old world order was still very much in business.

The brazenness of your death tempered the advance and

spawned a new guilt industry – Corporate Social Responsibility. The notion that, left to their own devices, corporations will act as good corporate citizens, is an interesting one, not least because while CSR was being loudly trumpeted, expensively advertised and propped up by an artifice of voluntary codes and offered as a sap to its critics, corporations were busy showing their true hand by working through GATT (General Agreements on Tariffs and Trade) negotiations, trying to install the Multilateral Agreement on Investment (MAI) and, subsequently, through the undemo-cratic offices of the WTO (World Trade Organisation).

The corporate agenda has a bewildering array of blunt international instruments, organisations and scholarship to advance and promote its cause. And yet, despite their supposedly good intentions expressed in the form of scholarships, grants, foundations and other PR activities, the world gets poorer as they pursue their real objectives: ever greater corporate wealth while the gap between the rich and poor is widening, wealth is being concentrated in ever-decreasing circles by the dictates of a commercial agenda that is self-serving and socially divisive.

Right now, we are in the middle of yet another expensive and troubling conflict in the Gulf. Lives are being lost daily in Iraq, which has been occupied on the pretext of something called the 'axis of evil' – a phrase which most people are now slowly coming to realise is really about access to oil. Because, since George Bush came to power – no, not the father but the son – the top five companies in the US have made $250 billion in clear profits. Imagine that – all the while the US has racked up record deficits to fight something called the 'War on Terrorism'. I won't bore you with the connections between Iraq and the War on Terrorism, but the shorthand of it goes something like this: 9/11 = Oil.

Don't worry if you don't understand the arithmetic, most people don't, but 70 per cent of Americans apparently understand that they have to fight a Holy War against a secular

Iraqi dictator and the Islamic fundamentalists from Saudi Arabia who killed 3000 people after flying planes into US buildings in Washington and New York.

If the riots in Seattle were a wake-up call to those who had forgotten the lessons of your death, then the war in Iraq is proving to be the morning after the night before. The second Gulf War may prove to be the defining moment for my generation, and generations to come, in working out how we can build an effective and global forum to balance the undoubted benefits that capitalism brings with a commitment to protect people and the planet.

That is the big picture; the little picture in Ogoni remains the more pressing issue for me because, despite all the international resolutions and the spotlight on Shell and Nigeria, nothing has changed materially at home. We are still impoverished; we are still waiting for an objective audit of the environment and a clean-up. Moreover, no-one has been held to account for the deaths and the rapes and the torture of Ogoni despite a UN resolution in 1996 to compensate the victims. You are still described as a murderer on Nigeria's statute books – even though your old friend General Olusegun Obasanjo is now president of a civilian regime. President Obasanjo even told me that your name should be hallowed in Nigeria.

But, as they say, a prophet is 'without honour in his own country'.

What I find heroic in all this is that, although we should be angry, our people remain committed to the non-violent methods you advocated. Not everyone in the Niger Delta agrees however; some groups have taken up the struggle, stepping into the vacuum created by your murder and decided that force must be met with force. Every day, the newspapers carry stories of kidnappings of foreign oil workers, pipelines being vandalised. There is a roaring trade in small arms in the Niger Delta – four guns to every computer. Much of the weaponry is coming out of the proceeds of oil bunkering. Crude oil is now trading above $65, would you believe! I think I need to go back and read your essay on 'The Coming War in the Delta' not least because I have returned home to keep an eye on the other parts of your legacy.

Sometimes I wonder about the sanity of the oil industry; why they never listened when you warned them that they would come to appreciate that you were, in fact, their best friend. But no; they continue to insist no quarter be given to environmental concerns and social principles. I can only imagine it is because they feel protected by governments and the military establishments – and that encourages them to continue with business as usual.

I keep hearing your death has changed corporate culture, but most of what I have seen – or, at least, have been allowed to see seems cosmetic. I suppose big organisations are like an oil tanker, changing direction is a slow process.

Whenever I get depressed by all this I think of the narrative arc of what you achieved; you took a small, unknown community and placed it firmly on the map of the world and in the world's conscience. Almost everywhere I travel these days – at a rally for a Burmese activist in Canada, in the jungles of Brazil, at a border crossing between the US and Canada – there are people who tell me that you inspired them. It took 30 years of tireless campaigning for you to achieve this. You did it all and still educated seven children, travelled the world, wrote several books and built a successful business. I am ever impressed and inspired by your example. Where I was once intimidated, I now see your achievements as a wonderful legacy to preserve and build on.

I often find the inspiration to keep on in the letters you wrote, in the books you have written, the buildings, the businesses, the commas and question marks of your story; it is these things that serve as a reminder of what is possible, and how. So when you say, in a video I just saw last week, that there is hope, I feel myself nodding enthusiastically. You really have taught me about what can be achieved. I can see that it is still possible to hope for – and, more importantly, to work towards – rebuilding the trust between minority communities, corporations and nation-states.

I can see that it is a long, often thankless and sometimes unforgiving road, with many bandits on the way. Sometimes, when I contemplate the size of the task, it seems so much more convenient to forget about all this. But then I remember how I tried to forget – it helped me to come to terms with your death for a while, but it was hard to continue to forget with the usual suspects dancing on your grave and trying to pervert your memory with their expensive lies about you. It is so outrageous, even if it is a backhanded compliment – that the consciences of so many people continue to be troubled by and exercised about Ken Saro-Wiwa. But as Milan Kundera once wrote 'the struggle of humanity against power is the struggle of memory against forgetting.'

That has become the motto of the tenth anniversary celebrations to commemorate your struggle and celebrate your life. The struggle continues – so your life, your work continues. You have three grandsons now and, despite everything that has happened to us, the family has just about survived. We have all endured our pain – especially those who have borne their anguish in private. No matter how we have dealt with this, I can say we have all carried it with the dignity that you would have expected from us.

Of course, it has not been easy; and who knows how your death may haunt generations of Wiwas and Saro-Wiwas to come? But least for now, we can hold our heads high. Your conscience should be clear, and you should be proud of us as we are all proud of you.

Jeje, Rest In Peace

Your Son